Social Skills for Teens

How to Build Self-Esteem, Confidence, and
Become Your Best Self

D1571935

By: Discover Press

Table of Contents

Introduction

The teen years are among the toughest times of most people's lives. You know that's true because you're *living* them. Are you ever confused or upset because of stuff that happens with your friends? Of course. Everybody says, "You'll get over it." What do they know? They don't know what it's like living inside of you. They don't feel what you feel. They don't think what you think. They don't have to worry about the future. They don't have crystal balls...or ones that really work!

You're an amazing person, although you may not always feel that way. You are unique, and no one else in the world is like you. Believe it or not, you can discover power and happiness just like a lot of others. It just takes a little effort, but it's fun. The fun is in the process of forging the kind of person you want to be and **know** you can be.

In this book, you will find little-known techniques for handling the challenges you face. This book can tell you things that you never knew before—things that not even your friends, your parents, or even your teachers know. It is a book written by those who know what it was like being anxious, being sad, and being very, very happy as a teen.

In this book, there is a way to discover the personality type you are, along with some advice as to how to navigate the waters of life. Wouldn't that be interesting? In here, there are true stories about other teens, their troubles, and their "wild 'n' crazy" times. You've all seen kids like that.

The other topics covered:

- Bullies
- Breasts
- Drugs
- Alcohol
- Your First Jobs
- Stranded Without Money
- Playing Hooky
- Building Self-Confidence
- Being Assertive

This book is written because people care about you. It's not meant to be "preachy" and isn't meant to sound that way. It's not written by perfect people who lived perfect lives. Life would sure be dull without its clumsy idiots, its clowns, those who drive you crazy, and those brainless wonders who claim to know everything about everything!

Chapter 1 – What Do They Think About Me?

You have the greatest challenge ever dealt out to a human being. You FEEL everything more deeply than your mother, your father, and your pesky brothers and sisters. "You'll get over it," your parents say. What garbage is that? You live in the "here and now." Besides, times were different then. Parents have long since forgotten what it feels like living inside themselves. They're not hit from every corner by the enormous flood of information pouring in from moment to moment. The latest crazy videos or that rotten kid on the social media site you would otherwise like to attend. The show-offs, the "better-than-thous," the weird guy who sits in the back of the class making strange nose noises, and those nasty kids who ignore you totally whenever you see them. You know how they're always accompanied by their "bodyguards" and faithful worshippers. And if you're a guy, how come so many of the others are bigger and taller than you are? How come the other girls look like they stepped off the cover of a beauty magazine? You feel like you're on trial by your own peers. It isn't fair. It's hard to pull off acting like someone else because you know deep down you'll be "discovered." Halloween only comes once a year—too bad.

So how come you can't show the confidence that Miley Cyrus shows? How come you can't be as popular as Bruno Mars? You just got invited to your first party in your new school and would love to stride in with your head held high like one of those stars. Well, you're going to try anyway. So you go to the door and ring the bell. The door opens and you don't even have a chance to look at the person who opened the door. They swung their head around when someone shouted and there you are…all alone on the threshold to your future. Miley Cyrus wouldn't have ever been subjected to such silence.

The Unwritten Code for Teens

Being a teen is tough. Human beings are, by nature, social. Everybody knows that, but for a teen, sometimes it seems to be the *most* important thing. It's a stringent law. Your little brother doesn't worry about it. ***But, as far as you're concerned, you have a desperate need to be liked and loved.*** No longer can Mom and Dad or your grandparents fill that role. They're *old*…They don't understand what it's like to be bombarded daily with advertising that tells you to be super-skinny, or muscular (if you're a guy), wear the latest fashions (if you can afford them), go to lots of parties (if your parents even let you), do your chores at home (yuck!), feed the dog who won't leave you alone, and get good grades (if you have time left over after all that other stuff to study!).

The respected psychologist, Abraham Maslow, rated the need for the esteem of others very high on his scale of human needs. As a teen, that need seems to be all-consuming because you're involved in figuring out what kind of person you are in the eyes of others and what kind of a person you'll be as an adult. You might feel very sensitive, and you can't always figure out what to do to attract **good** friends—the kind you can trust and will help you feel OK as a person. Maybe you often feel like you "don't fit in," or maybe you feel overwhelmed if all the others you know keep looking toward you to keep them entertained. If you slip up, some of those friends you met are gone with the wind! They're called "fair-weather friends" and not the *good* friends you want anyway.

Personality Types

Have you ever wondered what type of personality you have? That makes a tremendous difference in terms of developing your social skills, which seems to be of paramount importance as a teen. The mother-daughter team of psychologists, Isabel Meyers and Katherine Briggs, developed a test based on the personality classifications first delineated by the respected psychologist, Carl Jung. It's available on the Internet and will give you some valuable insights into how you can more comfortably relate to your peers. Knowing your personality type doesn't automatically bring fame and fortune, but knowing which one you're most like will give you an insight into your greatest strengths.

**Hold on to the personality descriptions presented by the Meyers-Briggs test. Keep in mind that the names they have assigned to them, for example "Inspector," doesn't mean you will be an inspector, per se. It just means that some of the qualities held by a person in charge might match some of your strengths.

We are going to consider the two major descriptions—introversion and extroversion first.

Are You Shy?

According to Meyers and Briggs, about half the world is what's called introverted. The dictionary says an introvert "is a person predominantly concerned with their own thoughts and feelings rather than with external things." Is that selfish?

No, not if half the world is like that, and it is. George Washington and Henry Ford, who developed the first assembly line, were introverts. Both were famous, so being an introvert doesn't mean you're a loser. They both were rich, too! There are some rewards for being introverted—and besides, the world benefits from people who think and feel a lot.

Let's say that a girl named Frederica at your school took the Meyers-Briggs test, and Frederica was what was called the "Architect Type." She was classified as an introvert. All the kids thought she was kind of "different," to use a polite expression. Frederica had just a couple of friends...not many like a lot of the other girls.

Frederica the "Fish"

Frederica arrived in the cafeteria with a plastic bag. Suddenly, she wasn't her usual quiet self. She was passing out shells—fantastic shells like you buy in the shops at the store. "Where did you get these?" they asked her. She explained in her usual "brainy" way that she went scuba diving over the summer with a couple of professional marine biologists. On and on, she raved about the bright

---

yellow angelfish that followed her around a Caribbean bay. "Some of them," she said, "nibbled at my backside!" Then she showed the others pictures of green moray eels which, she said, came popping out from holes in the coral reef, with their mouths open! Frederica then explained how she swam under some underwater rocks and saw tiny crayfish, with their dainty tenacles flying up in the water. It was an exciting trip, and Frederica attracted a lot of interest.

The "Architect Type" didn't mean Frederica was destined to be an architect, nor a scuba diver, for that matter, but she displayed the qualities of a high degree of self-confidence and the fact that she understood abstract concepts very well. She was very intellectual most of the time but was also very judgmental and fussy.

After being so shy most times, Frederica brightened up when she could tell others about her Caribbean adventure. It made her feel better about herself, as her abilities were recognized. Sometimes, an introverted person needs to share their experiences and thoughts with others. They don't have to be so quiet. Arnold Schwarzenegger, the actor and politician, is one of those personality types.

It is normal to think negatively about ourselves. For reasons unknown, we tend to dwell upon the negative first. It comes from the most basic of human instincts—self-survival. As a teen, you have a heightened sensitivity regarding the esteem of others. That, too, is a basic human need. We were born to be social, yet we tend to be more critical of ourselves than anyone else.

If so, you've created standards for yourself far above those of your other peers. When you rush to your favorite social media site, you're looking for acceptance. Have you ever noticed that—on that social media site—most people don't respond to each other? They may talk about some TV star or a singer, but very few people respond to each other with a compliment or observation. Take a close look next time. One by one, everybody pops on and says something about—guess who—themselves! Wow! They're just as hungry as you are looking for acceptance! Don't be astonished. This is perfectly normal, especially during your tender teenage years.

What about you? You are awesome, you know; but maybe you don't realize or believe it yet. Here's an exercise for you.

1. Call a friend, and ask him/her about themselves. Follow up with more questions.

2. Talk about one of your teachers, but be sure to ask him/her about what they think.

3. Ask about what things others do on their weekends, and follow up with more questions.

4. Suggest that they go with you to the mall and hang out. Before you know it, the other person will want to bring friends. Great!

5. Try an ice cream or coffee shop.

6. Find a recipe, and invite your friend over to try it out.

7. Have you done something at home to help out? Maybe you could help your brother with his homework.

8. Have you joined some extracurricular activities? Try one. Select something non-threatening.

9. Take a walk for a few blocks. Make it a point to wave "hello" to everybody. Watch how they smile back.

10. Think ahead of some topic you might be able to bring up to someone else around your age. Strike up a short conversation with that person.

Shy people sometimes come across as "stand-offish." If you're shy, remember that may be an impression others get about you. Introverts aren't that way at all. They "charge their batteries" by thinking and taking some time away from crowds.

Are You Outgoing?

Do you thrive on having a lot of friends? Are you spontaneous? Do you love parties? You're an extrovert whose interest lies in activities that are social, and you tend to be very active. You hate studying and find it difficult to force yourself to sit down to study for a test. Sometimes, though, you get terrific ideas and do especially well on your essay questions...except for the spelling. You don't want to waste time trying to look up proper spellings. That's a real drag.

Former U.S. President, Bill Clinton is an extrovert. That doesn't mean you're destined to be president, and maybe you don't want to be anyway. However, Clinton's administration was a prosperous one and he became highly respected and successful. His popularity, though, always depended upon other people. That can change. However, if he's popular with himself, that's different. The same thing goes for you. Be popular with yourself. <u>You are your own best</u>

friend.

Suppose you like to make people laugh and the teachers call you the "class clown." Even though you're outgoing, others may wander off to do something they feel is more interesting. That may make you feel bad. Shy people aren't the only ones who have problems—so do outgoing people.

Shawn the Coach

Shawn, who's usually with the other guys, wandered to the town park one day. There were a bunch of younger kids there who were trying to toss around a football but weren't doing too well. Shawn was an excellent football player, so he stood around watching them for a while. The ball was a pathetic thing, so Shawn interrupted them and told them he could make it easier to pass and kick. Obediently, the kids followed him to his garage, and he pulled out a pump, showed them how it worked, and pumped up the ball. They squealed with delight as they ran back to the field. Patiently, Shawn showed them how to kick the football so that it soared. He also taught them how to play "touch football" so they wouldn't get hurt...at least not too much. "This isn't played like the games on TV," he explained, "because you

---

don't have all that protective gear on." They then proceeded with the game. Shawn told them he would keep score, but he deliberately didn't. After all, these were just little kids. Shawn was a compassionate kind of guy, and he knew what it was like to lose. After he called the game over, he told them the score was even and said he'd give them all a soda from his garage.

Later on, one of the boys' fathers came over and suggested that Shawn become his assistant coach. Shawn was, of course, thrilled and had himself an activity for some of those long afternoons.

When the football season was over, Shawn didn't have his team anymore and missed them.

What you've noticed in the story is the fact that this kind of extrovert seems to constantly need other people around for him to feel OK. It also depresses him if he's alone. If you're like that, you may feel terrible about it, and it takes you a long time to get over it. Shawn took the Meyers-Briggs test and he classified himself as the "Performer Type." Performers need an audience, but they also need to learn how to handle the times when the audience isn't there anymore.

Whether you're shy or outgoing, it hurts you in particular when people are critical. You *hate* it, as a matter of fact, and you need some time to get over it. That's OK! However, in life that will happen, so it's important that you try and practice this next exercise in a safe environment.

Exercise for an outgoing person:

1. If there is one person to whom you feel closer, ask him or her to join a sports team in your town. Select a sport you haven't tried before, or don't have much experience with. Talk your friend into joining up with you and take the leap!

    Because you're not well-accomplished in that sport, you're not going to be the best, and your coach is going to make suggestions for change. This is the hard part. Follow the coach's instructions as best you can. *WHATEVER YOU DO...DON'T QUIT!* When you go home after that happens, share your feelings with your close friend.

    This practice is important to your future. There are many young people who are critical of how the boss wants things done, or they simply don't like them. Then they quit and get another job. Then they quit again and get another job. Then they quit yet again! And again…and again. When they get through a couple of years in college and apply for a job, they record their job history. No potential employer is impressed if your work history shows a whole series of short-lived jobs. That will reduce your employability, and you may have to settle for a low-level/entry-level position, not one that's ideally suited to your education.

2. As another alternative, join a debate team.

3. Form your own study club. Be sure to ask one or two of those "brainy" kids. Let the "brainy" kid contribute more than you do. That may be difficult for you to do, but the results will be far better, and you can benefit from taking "second place."

The above exercise has a reward for you. You are not just an outgoing person, but you do have the amazing ability to draw people together and get them to work harmoniously.

Who Is "They"?

Do you ever feel like you don't "fit in?" Like you don't measure up to the standards of your peers? You've spent a fortune on the latest clothes and your parents are yelling at you because they're not going to keep loaning you money for more. They won't let you go to a concert. "Everybody else is going," you complain. You feel odd because you are a little overweight, or you're not muscular enough to compete with the jocks. You get on your favorite social media site, say something, and everybody ignores you.

If you're the outgoing type of person, how do you feel when not everybody responds? You want to be the person who starts the new trends. When you're alone, you miss all your friends. Your sense of self-worth depends upon what *"they"* think of you. You hate to disagree with them, but then *"they"* say you're inconsistent and keep changing your mind. It's the great god *"they"* who dictates how you're supposed to behave, what you're supposed to say, and what you're supposed to do. If you're not sure how *"they"* feel about you, you're uncomfortable.

There is a Creed that *"they"* say you HAVE to follow to be successful. Who are *"they"*? *"They"* are the great invisible ogre who dictates the behavior of "everybody else." *"They"* are those popular kids who text constantly throughout math class. *"They"* are those girls with long, shiny hair who show their cleavage and make it a point to bend down in front of the good-looking guys.

"They" is everybody but you, or so you may think. That makes you feel bad, doesn't it?

What are the rules you're supposed to follow to be popular and successful? Those rules aren't the ones made up by the teachers or your parents. The Creed is something all of you know, but neither you nor your friends have a clue about who wrote it.

The Creed of They

1. You're supposed to know who the latest pop singers and rap artists are.
2. You're supposed to party a lot and maybe even sneak in a little beer to the party.
3. You're supposed to be good at athletics or as a cheerleader.
4. You're supposed to know the latest styles and wear them, but not twice in a row.

---

5. It's OK if you have to go to summer school so you don't have to study too hard. Even the popular kids have to go.

6. You have to have a girlfriend or boyfriend.

7. You have to hang out with the other kids at the mall or down the street.

8. You're supposed to have an impressive Facebook page with lots and lots of friends. You're also supposed to contribute to Twitter and Instagram regularly.

9. You're supposed to have answers when teachers call upon you. If you don't know the answer, you're supposed to make a joke of it.

10. You're supposed to be skinny if you're a girl and muscular if you're a boy.

11. If you're a girl, you're supposed to have long straight hair parted in the middle. If you're a guy, you're supposed to have hair on your chest and great biceps.

12. You're never supposed to be seen with your parents or your kid brother or sister.

13. If you're a girl, you're supposed to have very attractive fingernails.

No one has the right to tell you that you have to do all those things or be all those things. It's not the law. It's some belief schedule set up by an invisible force. The great "they" didn't ask you what you think or how you feel. You have a free will. You are the only person who can decide what you will do. That Creed isn't the law. You can do some of those things in the so-called "Creed," but only if you want to.

"Comparisons Are Odious"

The above phrase was created way back in the 15th century but still works today. Many things change, but some things always remain the same. "Comparisons are odious" means that comparing two things or people and expecting close similarities is foolish. By their nature, people are different. They have different responses, have different preferences, look good in different clothes, and have different body shapes. You and your younger brother or sister are different even though you have the same parents.

Have you ever noticed the clothing rack in the changing room at a department store? There are hundreds of rejected clothes hanging there. No two people are similar. Not even size 8 fits the same way on two different women who wear that size.

23

Have you ever noticed a heavy teen trying to squeeze into tight clothes that show every bump and bulge on her body? And then—guess what—she buys it! Why? Because she's following the Creed of "they."

Jeff Bezos, the founder of Amazon, addressed that issue when he said, "Will you follow dogma, or will you be original? Will you choose a life of ease or a life of service and adventure? Will you wilt under criticism, or will you follow your convictions? Will you bluff it out when you are wrong, or will you apologize?" Jeff Bezos is a billionaire who followed his own beliefs and fulfilled his own dreams. Those dreams weren't the same as those of everyone else. Yet, he took his chances and ventured out into his own life. No doubt, he was hesitant at first (although he may not have told you). He didn't tell you about all the *other* ideas he had before he developed Amazon. Perhaps they didn't work out, but he didn't stop trying.

Another billionaire, the late Steve Jobs, started that huge telecommunication company, Apple. He once said, "Don't waste time living someone else's life."

The noise all those teens make about clothes, looks, and entertaining an intense desire to be popular can drown out your own inner voice who whispers about *WHO YOU ARE*.

The Masks

The kids in school are very fond of being like everyone else, so they try to act like the popular kid, assuming it will attract many friends and bring success. Are you sure you want to pretend to be someone else? People can see right through that, and you'll be labeled as "fake." This isn't Halloween. If you wear a "mask," no one will know who you really are and won't know what to expect of you. They won't trust you. Every friendship is built on trust.

If you try to conform to the expected teenage norms, you won't like yourself. The mask you've chosen just doesn't fit.

Chapter 2 – Who Am I?

The famous writer and novelist, Oscar Wilde, once said, "Be yourself. Everybody else is already taken!" Funny…but true. It takes tremendous courage to be who you really are. Because you've spent so much time trying to be like the others, sometimes you can lose sight of that which makes you unique. Take a look at your favorite singers. *None* of them sings the same way. Every single show they put on is very, very different from other shows. Each singer or group has an entirely different style, and their uniqueness attributes to their success.

If you took the Meyers-Briggs test cited at the beginning of this book, refer now to the descriptions of personality types. It will give you an idea of the strengths (and weaknesses) you may have. However, keep in mind that you are a "work-in-progress." You may very well have many of the strengths listed, but haven't yet developed them.

Description Exercise #1 – This first exercise may feel negative, but let's face it—one's weaknesses are the first to come to mind when a person describes himself or herself.

Your Weaknesses

1. Make a list of 10 to 12 weaknesses you believe you have.

2. Make a list of 10 to 12 people who are famous and well-known, but who appear to have similar weaknesses. They can just be a character on a TV show if you wish. If you can't think of that many famous people with those weaknesses, just leave those lines blank.

Description Exercise #2 – The second exercise is positive. However, it will take you much longer to do this one than Exercise #1.

Your Strengths

1. Make a list of 10 to 12 strengths you believe you have. This can include academic smarts, chores you do around the house regularly, favors you do for your friends, physical prowess, cooking or artistic/craft/writing talents, socializing skills, and the like.

> 2. Make a list of 10 to 12 people who are famous or whom you know who have similar abilities and strengths.

Note: When you're a teen, you haven't yet "found" yourself. You cannot help but compare yourself with those you consider popular, good-looking, smart, or successful. You are going to be "down" on yourself. This is normal at your age, and the teen years will be the most stressful parts of your life. Your parents, too, are living that stress with you. You see, your parents also have their own ideas about how you should behave, what you should wear, what kind of grades you should get at school, and a whole litany more. That's because they want what's best for you, but are sometimes just as confused as you are in terms of the kind of adult you're destined to become, and fear the worst. They may also feel guilty that they didn't raise you well if you get into trouble. Arguments are common between teens and parents, and that's uncomfortable for all of you.

Hints: If you're stumped, look at this list. Perhaps you can add some of these strengths to your list:

Trustworthy

Caring

Lively

Intelligent

Serious

Organized

Determined

Friendly

Practical

Appreciative

Enjoys making jokes

Physically active

Straightforward

Patient

Idealistic

Honest

Flexible

Ambitious

Description Exercise #3 – This exercise maybe even harder than the other two. It takes intuition and self-knowledge to do it. List some things you can do that are "weird" or different...something most or all other people can't do.

My Weird Skills

Perhaps you can imitate the voice of a cartoon character. Maybe you can walk on your hands. Perhaps you're an expert at skateboarding. Can you make weird faces? Tell ghost stories? Paint murals on walls of an old brick building? Talk with your mouth closed? Do you raise lizards or snakes? Do you work on old cars?

When he was eight-years-old, an adopted boy who grew up in Dallas, Texas, received a Mortimer Snerd dummy at Christmas. He played with it, then checked out a book on ventriloquism from the local library. He felt he would like to become a professional ventriloquist. When he became a teenager, he got a job working at *Six Flags* (Great Adventure). While he was there, his employer let him perform at a banquet held for the Dallas Cowboys. In his yearbook, he posed for photos along with the puppets he'd collected by that time. He attended Baylor University and performed around campus. After graduation, he was asked to perform for General Electric and started to become very well-known. What he had done was to put effort, study, and much practice into developing the weird skill of ventriloquism. He was finally able to get a gig at the nightclub, *Catch a Rising Star*, but was derided by the management, as ventriloquism wasn't a respected comedy routine. His act was postponed and postponed until he quit trying and then moved to Los Angeles, hoping for the best. His show in Los Angeles bombed! His status as a ventriloquist wasn't respected. His parents were very concerned and assumed he and his puppets would be relegated to local shows back home at Church bazaars in Texas. At that time, he admitted he had never held a "real job." Someone then finally offered him some solid advice and told him his script-writing was poor. That was no doubt a painful criticism but was enlightening.

He then studied the styles of popular comedians like Jerry Seinfeld. He continued to work on his skill and was able to appear on more comedy shows, including Johnny Carson, but his career was stop-and-go until about ten years later. Who is he? Jeff Dunham!

Jeff Dunham is an example of someone who learned who he was at a young age and developed a flourishing career out of his unique skills. Although you may not become famous, you can still become happy and successful—but it is built upon your uniqueness as a person, not the conformity you adhered to as a teen. Who you will be as an adult is also built upon your strengths. So will be your eventual career.

Love Yourself

Malcolm Forbes, a wealthy entrepreneur, once said, "Too many people overvalue what they are not and undervalue what they are." When we were born, we automatically loved ourselves. Your parents sure knew that each time you cried in a voice that could wake the neighborhood when you wanted one of them to pick you up and cuddle you a bit. It is natural to love yourself and to be your own best friend. So, what happened? The peers, the teachers, the rules, and the behaviors expected of courtesy. Now that you're a teen, it seems everybody is struggling to be recognized for who they are. But you, as one person who has not reached their full potential, aren't sure who that might be.

This is one of the most challenging phases of your young life, and you're to be applauded for beginning that journey by reading this book and exploring all the possibilities that are ahead of you. Many do not, you know. They just plow through school and somehow end up in college—perhaps without any clear goals in life because they haven't come to terms with their strengths and their weaknesses, as well as their dreams and aspirations. They sign up for college courses with little or no knowledge of what they want to do with their lives, so they take courses that sound easy or whatever the college counselors tell them they have to take. Again, the Creed of They has taken over their lives. Try taking a free career test on the Internet. Don't take the results as absolute fact, but it may stimulate some thoughts as to how your strengths will give you direction in life.

The Pleasure Hormones

The brain is run by neurotransmitters or a psychologically stimulated series of impulses from one neuron (brain cell) to another. Two of those hormones, oxytocin and the DHEA hormone, urge you to feel content with yourself. Cohen and Greene, as well as Rilling et. al., of Emory University conducted studies related to those two hormones. Their studies proved that self-love was natural, as it was naturally produced by the brain. For those who are plagued by anxiety, those two hormones reduce another hormone responsible for stress and weight gain—cortisol. Cortisol is the stress hormone and comes in handy when you need an extra jolt of energy if a half-crazed raccoon comes racing toward you some eerie evening. It's not so handy when you start feeling sorry for yourself, go to the refrigerator, and eat a bunch of snacks in a misguided effort to make yourself feel better.

Plan on finding something funny to read or to share with your friends every day. Here's one that's quite amusing and appeared one time in a newspaper:

"Charges were filed against a man who showed up at a police station in a bunny costume blasting an air horn...Charges were filed because he purposely alarmed the dispatchers."

Humor is a life-saver. Everybody likes to laugh, and it takes the curse off the difficult times you have to weather through. Then your comfort hormones will rage through your arteries and veins.

Jump in While the Water's Cold!

When you were younger, you had a routine. The blessing of routines is the fact that they provide security. That gives you a sense of calmness, and you always know what to expect. When you become a teen, you have to get used to new class schedules, new kids, and perhaps even new subjects you want nothing to do with. It can build up anxiety and raw feelings.

True Story: Mitchell the Voice

Mitchell was a skinny boy who always compensated for his feelings of inferiority with his voice. He got into trouble a lot because he was a thief. He stole jackets, gold necklaces for his girlfriend, and bikes. When confronted about those thefts, he used his favorite defense—his voice. Mitchell could holler loud enough to frighten five classrooms full of kids until they got used to it.

Whenever he got caught stealing, he LOUDLY denied it! One day, Mitchell was in the office of the school social worker. Oddly enough, he wasn't there on account of stealing anything this time. The social worker had to see him about some changes in his class schedule. Suddenly, Mitchell became very upset about that and let loose a blood-curdling holler. The principal, the school nurse, and the secretary came racing in. "What's the problem?" they asked.

"I CAN'T STAND ALL THESE CHANGES! I CAN'T TAKE IT ANYMORE!" he screamed, leaping up with his fists clenched.

It took Michell half an hour to calm down. Yet, overtly, a

change of class schedule wouldn't seem to be traumatic. However, for Mitchell, it was. Why?

When you become upset or nervous, a hormone called adrenaline will race up from your adrenal glands above your kidneys. It flies straight to your brain and prepares you for action. Adrenaline gives rise to the "fight-flight-freeze" response. It's very useful if you're confronted by a nasty kid who's threatened you. In Mitchell's case, his response didn't suit the trigger—a change of schedule—but he felt like he wanted to punch somebody out anyway. Mitchell had an extreme reaction, and you can also have a powerful reaction when you have to deal with something uncomfortable. (Hopefully, you won't respond as forcefully as Mitchell!)

Times are changing in your teens, and incidentally, so are you. Your carefully laid-out plans most likely won't come out the way you pictured them. Life has a nagging way of being spontaneous. You will have to take time out to remind yourself that you are OK.

Exercise: Try venturing out of our ordinary behaviors and activities. Get used to functioning outside your comfort zone. Try joining a sports team or the glee club, try talking to someone you never spoke to before, make a post on a new social media site, upload a vlog on YouTube, or invite someone new to join you and your friends at the mall or wherever you like to hang out.

Affirmations

At times when you feel uncomfortable and unsure of yourself, review these affirmations to reinforce your sense of well-being and comfort with yourself:

1. I approve of myself. I am a good person.
2. I will always walk forward and let the shadows of the past fall behind me. (Picture yourself doing that.)
3. Although it may be hard, I will summon up the power I have within myself.
4. I can and will deal with the changes coming up in my life.
5. Every day will bring new opportunities for change and growth.
6. I deserve respect and the admiration of others, especially those younger than me.
7. I am grateful for all the good things that have already happened in my life.
8. I am smart enough to figure things out for myself, and

have the courage to ask for advice if I need it.

9. I can and will accomplish my goals.

10. I am mature enough to take responsibility for my life for what was good and what didn't turn out that well.

Avoid the Status Quo

The "Status Quo" means the state of life and living as it is now. It is opposite to the way things can be in the future. If all goes as would be expected, you're going to change. However, some teens resist change, like the story of Mitchell discussed above. Look at the other teens around you. Do you know any of them who act immature? They might want to be stuck with childish things. Life for them is predictable, but they're not likely to become highly-motivated and successful adults. What if Jeff Dunham quit after his show bombed in Los Angeles? He kept changing and was willing to grow. Ben Stein, a comedian, actor, and political commentator once said, "So many fail because they don't get started—they don't overcome inertia. They don't begin."

The temptation of inertia sets in every morning when the alarm clock goes off. It often elicits a moan and the challenge of facing another day. You know change won't happen if you stay in bed. But as teens, those hormones will kick up (whether you like it or not) and you'll be driven to make tomorrow better than yesterday- or maybe you'll be afraid that tomorrow will be worse than yesterday.

Inertia will result in negative feelings about yourself. It can cause you to:

- Lie around and watch TV all-day
- Read new posts on social media and fail to contribute
- Eat and eat
- Procrastinate
- Play computer games
- Mull around the neighborhood

It's safer to hide in the fog of inertia because it hides you from the feelings of discomfort that accompany growth and change.

For you to become the person you want to be, you need to venture out of your comfort zone. You need to "jump in while the water is cold," and you'll be a far better person for doing it.

Thoughts and Feelings

You've read all that's written above and understand it clearly, don't you? Then how come the rest doesn't come easily? The poet Edna St. Vincent Millay said it very well: "Pity me that the heart is slow to learn what the swift mind beholds at every turn." Yes, it's those "pesky" emotions that crop up to fog up the windshield of our minds. The mind works in concert with your emotions, but emotions are powerful at influencing behavior. As you move through your teenage years, the emotions of anxiety and depression will sometimes overcome you. An imbalance of the hormone serotonin can trigger feelings of depression. The psychologist, Daniel Goleman, used the term "Emotional IQ," meaning that people with a high Emotional IQ have learned to control their emotions with the help of their higher brain centers. When you summon your higher brain, you can learn to label your emotions. Something as simple as forcing yourself to smile will release a hormone called "GABA." That can stimulate mental relaxation, help reduce depression, and reduce anxiety and stress.

You and other teens are going through a period of emotional chaos and inner turmoil. You're young and just learning how to deal with those feelings in such a way that you don't ignore them by surrendering to the Status Quo, but moving into new unfamiliar territory outside your comfort zone. Most of you have been tossed around in that uncomfortable wilderness, but control of the journey is the surest way to reach your full potential. All of you, without exception, want to become that person. You are already a good person, but can be far better than who you are today.

Most of us have a negative bias. It's natural to the human being who has their first focus upon his/her survival needs. The first thing humans have been hard-wired to do is protect the self from any harmful external stimuli that happen their way. It resides in the animal part of us. Did you know that birds of different species communicate with each other in times of crisis? When wild birds are nesting and there are eggs in their nests, the strongest of them—regardless of what kind of birds they are—fly through the air sounding out an alarm call when predators are about. They make a particular sound when a cat is prowling about, as a matter of fact! They also have been known to attack the offending cat, chasing it out of a backyard!

Feelings are difficult to control, but you'd be a robot without them. If you could simply go through life without those unruly feelings, where would be the joy in that? There are people who don't express their feelings. They really do have feelings, but their capacity to experience them is very low. They've been called "asocial" personalities. Maybe they can breeze through their tumultuous teens with no problems.... No—wait! They can't because they don't get through the teens unscathed by the experience. Take, for example, the story of Stella.

True Story: Stella the Stoic

Stella was the smartest girl in her first year of junior high. She never did anything wrong. She had planned on becoming a mathematics teacher. At home, she was a model young lady...took care of her chores and enjoyed spending time in the park every day. She was elected class president.

Stella seemed to be the epitome of perfection. She was in the glee club and was a gymnast. However, Stella was just "too good to be true." She never reacted to anything emotionally, was always well-controlled and sensible.

One day, the girl in the seat next to her decided to try to play a trick on her. The girl just couldn't resist. Because Stella was the only one paying any attention during geometry class,

---

she always raced up to erase the blackboard for the teacher. Every time she did so, her companion removed something from her desk. One by one things left: her tablet, her notepad, her pens, her cell phone, her purse, and her papers until the desk was empty. The teacher then noticed and seemed shocked. Stella still said nothing.

It was clear Stella was rattled and was made vulnerable by her peers, who giggled and tittered with delight when they saw the event.

Stella's reaction was a paralysis of sorts. She was always known as the good kid...the smart kid...someone who seemed to be perfect. However, her reactions weren't healthy ones. She played out the "freeze" phase of the "fight-flight-freeze" syndrome. She was wrapped up in her own terror, and hadn't yet learned how to stand up for herself. Stella's image had been shattered by one solitary event.

Her classmates also failed because they permitted Stella to go on feeling isolated and rejected. They failed in their sense of caring. As a teen, there may be times when you have these kinds of experiences. Sometimes, teens can be cruel. It is a reality, and in this case, the anxiety is justified. However,

Stella can learn to deal with it by performing relaxation exercises, like the one below.

Relaxation Exercise

When you are becoming flooded with an emotion, label where you feel it. The most common area is the midsection—the stomach or the abdomen. It could also be in your arms if you notice that they're tensing up.

- Sit in a comfortable chair and focus on the top of your head. Close your eyes slightly or cast them downward.

- Inhale through your nose and exhale through your mouth. Attempt to slow down your breathing little by little.

- Thoughts will intrude. Dismiss them, but do so gently. Tell yourself you'll think those thoughts later.

- Become aware of the noises from outside. Let them intrude, but dismiss each one of them.

- Focus upon your stomach area. Sense the rise and fall of your abdomen as you breathe slowly in and out.

- Let your arms dangle at your side. Imagine they're filled with sand. Then visualize the sand running out onto the floor.

- Relax in that position for a while. Little by little, permit yourself to become aware of the world around you.

- Rise slowly from the chair.

The above exercise is adapted from the mindfulness technique first introduced by Dr. Jon Kabat-Zinn who studied the techniques of the Eastern mystics. Studies throughout the years have proven that these kinds of exercises enhance positive emotions and reduce stress.

Chapter 3 – Anxiety

Did you know that the world would come to a halt without anxiety? Take a look at the diagram below. It pictures the Yin and Yang, the ancient Chinese principles describing how two opposing forces can be complementary. Imagine the wheel you see below is rotating. There is a tension between the two forces. As one moves, it pushes the other, and together they create motion.

Imagine that one side signifies a restful state, and the other side is desire. Once a person is filled with desire, tension rises until the wheel starts to turn and the person moves toward the object of their desire. The wheel can turn the opposite way, and go backward to avoid the object they fear. The two opposites create a sense of tension or anxiety by which a person moves toward or away from the object. For example, a young woman looks longingly at a dress in the store window, and says to her friend, "I'm *anxious* to buy that dress as soon as I get the money." We tend to think of anxiety as negative, but all anxiety isn't bad. You see a cute boy (or girl) and are *anxious* to meet them, so you design some strategy or scenario by which you can meet them, as if casually. On the other hand, if you see someone in the distance who always gives you a hard time, you cross the street or turn and go down the side street. You're *anxious* to get away from that person. You're stressed out.

In the 21st century, you experience a lot more stress than the teens of twenty years ago. The digital age has contributed a great deal to that. Sometimes you might feel that you have to keep up with *all* the new trends and the latest news. It isn't long before you find out that it's impossible to do that because of the amount of advertising and the flood of information that comes your way daily. You don't want to miss out on the important items, so you're forced to choose between what you need to do to keep up and what you can eliminate.

In a study by the American Psychological Association two years ago, they discovered that 23% of teens skipped meals, 30% felt stressed out, and 36% felt tired most of the time. Many teens denied that anxiety and stress had any effect on their mental and physical health. Dr. Norman Anderson of the APA said, "It is concerning that they seem to underestimate the potential impact that stress has on their physical and mental health." It is crucial that you try to reduce your anxiety and stress using the techniques discussed in this book and elsewhere.

The Triggers

Your sense of self-awareness becomes stronger with age. You begin to use your mind to apprehend a situation. Then that gives rise to an emotive response. Dealing with negative anxiety is a tremendous challenge, as you cannot always avoid bad situations throughout life.

What triggers your negative anxieties? Keep a hidden journal or a diary as to what set you off during the day. Record what time of day it occurred and what you were doing before you became anxious and what happened afterward as well. At the end of a month, review it and analyze it for repeating patterns and settings. What kinds of events trigger the greatest anxieties within you?

How do you physically react when you're most anxious? Do you tense up? Are there butterflies in your stomach? Do you clench your fists? Vibrate and shake? Have faith. You can learn to quell those uncomfortable reactions, with patience.

Social Anxiety Disorder

If your symptoms are more serious, you may have what is called Social Anxiety Disorder. Don't be alarmed. This affects only a small handful, but it's still not a disaster. Its symptoms may include one or all of the following: a racing heart, a tingling sensation in your hands, and shortness of breath. If your symptoms disrupt your daily activities to the point that it interferes with your cognition, or if it feels like constant emotional "static" is going on in your head very frequently, don't feel embarrassed to approach a counselor or an older adult whom you know you can trust. This book can act as a steppingstone for you as well.

Words you think of in your own mind can have a POWERFUL IMPACT and act as a springboard for an explosion of negative emotions.

As you review your journal, circle the following words:

NEVER

ALWAYS

MAKES ME FEEL

HATE IT WHEN

SHOULDN'T

CAN'T

The above words are words often used by teens who unfortunately view themselves as victims. Although they're hardly obscenities, they're toxic for you to think. Those words are all absolutes and give the impression that someone or something else is controlling your thoughts and emotions. You're not going to let them!

Here is an example list of those toxic words that a girl named Tasha applied to herself:

1. I **never** go to parties. I get too nervous.

   _____

   _____

2. I **always** feel left out when a group of the girls go shopping in the mall.

   _____

   _____

   _____

   _____

3. Geraldine **makes me feel** inferior.

   _____

   _____

   _____

   _____

4. I **hate it when** the others whisper. I think they're making fun of me.

_____

_____

_____

_____

5. I **shouldn't** be late coming home.

_____

_____

6. I **can't** think of anything to say, so I tend not to talk to the other kids.

_____

_____

_____

_____

Exercise: Use the list above or use your own list from your journal. Carefully study each of your common thoughts when you list your anxious situations. What are your toxic, victim-like words?

Has it ever occurred to you that many of your assessments of events may be exaggerated, wrong, generalized, incorrect? Go through this list and/or your own and make clarifications. Note that, in every instance, you don't experience those situations 100% of the time. Here's what modifications Tasha made to her list of gripes:

1. I **never** go to parties. I get too nervous around other kids.

   Well, I went to Kathy's party. I baked some cupcakes for her. She's my closest friend.

   *Analysis: Tasha **does go** to parties, but is rather selective in deciding what people she associates with.*

2. I **always** feel left out when a group of the girls go shopping in the mall.

They don't actually say I can't come; they just leave for the mall and I go home.

*Analysis: Because she's very shy, Tasha **assumes** that the other girls don't want Tasha to join them. She thinks they don't like her. She could easily tag along. None of the girls are going to object.*

3. Geraldine **makes me feel** inferior.

   Geraldine is so vivacious. I could never compete with her.

Analysis: Tasha entertains the false belief that others expect her to be just like Geraldine. No doubt, the other girls probably can't compete with Geraldine either! Tasha has also made Geraldine responsible for her own negative feelings. Geraldine hasn't made Tasha feel anything.

Besides, the other girls are just letting Geraldine be herself. There is nothing wrong with that. It doesn't mean anything bad about Tasha.

4. I **hate it when** the others whisper. I think they're making fun of me.

   Well, I don't know for sure if they're talking about me.

Analysis: Tasha assumes that the others are talking about her. The only way she can verify that would be to summon up the courage to ask what they're talking about. Tasha would be quite surprised if she found out that the other girls were talking about a boy!

5. I **shouldn't** be late coming home.

   Usually, I'm late coming home, but I was right on time the last two days.

Analysis: Tasha isn't late 100% of the time, but it might be important to make an effort to be on time a little more often. Even so, being late isn't a "criminal offense!"

6. I **can't** think of anything to say, so I tend not to talk to the other kids.

   Well, I did ask Maura about her science project, 'cause she won a prize for it.

Analysis: Tasha here demonstrates a kindness by extending a compliment to Maura, and will receive gratitude for that recognition. Tasha did think of something to say after all.

If she didn't say anything, the other kids will just assume Tasha's a "quiet type." That's OK, you know.

Fact and Fiction

A lot of people, not merely teens, have a negative bias. Instead of basing their conclusions about an event on thought, they base their conclusions on their own emotions—emotions no one has expressed, mind you.

For example, a classmate walks down the street and doesn't greet you. Suppose you then jump to the conclusion they deliberately ignored you because deep down they don't want anyone to know you know them. Maybe the girl thinks you're weird, you tell yourself. Maybe she doesn't want you to talk to her, you think.

Take another look at the situation, and <u>separate fact from fiction:</u>

Fact: A classmate walks down the street and doesn't greet you.

Fiction: She deliberately ignored you.
Fiction: She doesn't want anyone to see you with her.
Fiction: You're weird.
Fiction: She doesn't think you deserve to be greeted.

ARE YOU A CLAIRVOYANT? DO YOU READ PEOPLE'S MINDS?

There could other plausible reasons the person didn't greet you. She could have been absorbed in thought about something else. It could be she's unaccustomed to seeing anyone she knows in that area, so she wasn't paying attention. Her feet could be killing her, and she's hoping to find a bench very, very soon! So, she was distracted.

It Isn't You!

All people, especially you teens, are somewhat oversensitive to the opinions of others. As the psychologist Abraham Maslow has said, everyone has a strong need for the esteem of others. As a tender teen, you seek it out avidly. You will tend to be overly alert to a look, a failure to look, facial expressions, or when another turns away from you.

Here is a truism: **Everyone** in a social group is thinking about the same thing you are! Each one of them is wondering how **they** are coming across to you and the group! They need the esteem of others as much as you do. They're more concerned with whether or not *you* like them! Smile a lot, and they'll smile back. It's automatic.

What about the person who has a negative expression on her face? Again, it's a question of fact and fiction.

Fact: Julie has a nasty grimace on her face.

Fiction: She's mad at me.
Fiction: She's annoyed I'm there.
Fiction: She wants to get away from me.

Here's what really happened:

The Triad

Julie, Natalie, and Sally were sitting nearby at their study period. Light conversation was allowed, as long as it had to do with schoolwork. Julie had her eyes glued to a book. Sally then asked to borrow her pen. Julie looked up, but had a 'nasty grimace' on her face. Sally jumped to the conclusion that Julie was mad at her. The three of them were then silent during the rest of the period.

When they went outside, Sally felt bad because she assumed she did something wrong to Julie, and was getting the 'silent treatment.' However, Natalie dared to ask Julie if she was upset. It took a long time, and a lot of coaxing, until Julie burst out crying and said that the teacher in the class right before this one embarrassed her in front of the whole class because she had done such a poor job on her homework.

Natalie summoned up her courage to confront the issue head-on. Overcoming anxiety often calls for the courage to face one's fears. It helps to keep a person focused on reality and eliminates misinterpretation. Your teenage years are difficult enough without creating imaginary problems you need to deal with.

The positive side-effect of the discussion of Julie's issue was two-fold: 1) the other two girls had an opportunity to feel empathic and give Julie some comfort, and 2) because she dared to bring up the issue verbally, Natalie became more self-confident and would most likely take more risks in the future to deal with uncomfortable issues head-on. Although Sally didn't bring up the issue, she learned that she had also misinterpreted the incident, and learned from Natalie's example that some events are best handled forthrightly.

Foods and Vitamins for Helping Alleviate Anxiety

Avoid alcohol. The initial effect of alcohol is relaxing, but it soon converts and becomes a stimulant. Caffeine is also not recommended. Many soft drinks come in a caffeine-free form. If you're a young coffee drinker, at least cut the regular coffee with decaf. Sugar, of course, should be kept to a minimum, unless it's artificial sugar such as what's sold today. NutraSweet, however, isn't recommended.

Magnesium is a very effective supplement, as it boosts the production of serotonin, the balancing hormone. If you prefer not to take it in pill form, you can eat it naturally in the following foods:

- Fish

- Spinach

- Seeds and nuts

- Barley, oats, quinoa, whole grain rice

- Bananas

- Dark chocolate (Yummy!)

- Avocados

- Fat-free yogurt

Vitamin B1 is also helpful, but you must not take an overdose of it. Take only as directed. Vitamin B doesn't break down in the body for quite some time. As an alternative, you can consume:

- Potatoes

- Carrots

- Broccoli

- Cauliflower

- Wheat (any form)

- Sunflower seeds (They're fun to suck on, and doing so tends to relax the body.)

- Peas

- Nuts and fish (also cited above)

No doubt, you've seen Uncle Joe doze off after Thanksgiving dinner. He is reacting to tryptophan, the well-known ingredient found in turkey. Of course, you can hardly suck on a turkey when you're anxious (!), but these foods will last longer in your body and do have sedative effects. Some are high in antioxidants which also have a calming effect:

- Sunflower seeds (also cited above)
- Pork
- White fish
- Soybeans (edamame)
- Blueberries
- Asparagus
- Blackberries
- Raisins
- Eggs
- Sweet potatoes
- Tomatoes

Homeopathic remedies that reduce anxiety have a time-honored history going back to the 18th century and Samuel Hahnemann, a German physician and the founder of homeopathy. They're derived from plant products, are organic, and can be found in many health food and vitamin stores:

- White chestnuts
- Homeopathic sulfur remedies
- Cherry plums
- Calcium carbonate in pill form

Chapter 4 – Building Self-Confidence

Girl Bullies and Boy Bullies

Bullying has unfortunately become a problem for many teens. Those of you who are bullied feel afraid, embarrassed, depressed, and powerless. Bullies say mean things, because they think that others will look up to them. Bullies often have friends with them that reinforce their tyrannical behaviors. They get a "kick" out of being bossy. Pretty sick, isn't it?

You don't have to let them bully you. Experts have made suggestions for how to best handle these obnoxious people.

1. Avoid the people who do the bullying. If it happens on the playground, look around for those girls or guys who are elsewhere. Just walk up to them and join their group. If you don't know them well, introduce yourself.

2. Some girls and guys seem to get some perverse pleasure in saying nasty things on your social media.

THEY'RE 'BAITING' YOU! These people are called "social media trolls." They are deliberately saying controversial things or making insulting remarks to get a rise out of others. Don't fall for it! Leave the site immediately, or block them if you can. What you have to say is fun; it's important and interesting. Find a more comfortable audience.

3. Develop at least one other friend and walk to class with him or her in the yard. Bullies tend to avoid groups of people who aren't their targets.

4. Ignore any bullying insults thrown at you. This is hard to do, because they will say things that may make you angry and you'll be tempted to respond or feel sorry for yourself. Remember this—bullies need an audience. Without an audience, they will get frustrated and go away.

5. Bullies tend to hang out in certain places—the water fountain, certain areas of the hall at school, a deli store downtown, or even in the bathrooms. Map out an escape route where you can slip by unseen.

6. If a bully confronts you face-to-face with an insulting remark, look at them directly. Don't stand too close to them, because you don't want them to hit you. Look at the bridge of their nose. To them it will appear as if you're looking directly into their eyes. STAY CALM. Pause, saying nothing. Then calmly say something to the effect of you don't appreciate what they're saying and you're not interested. Then turn and walk away. Keep ignoring them. Remember, a bully without an audience gives up and looks for another victim.

7. You can also report a bully's behavior to a counselor or your parents. When it's serious enough, it should be reported.

Here's an example of what once happened in a junior high school:

True Story: The Fifth Period Dilemma

Miss Marsh taught science in the junior high school. During her class one day, a boy asked to be excused to go to the bathroom. He returned. Soon after, another boy asked to be excused, and shortly returned. About five minutes later, another boy asked and then returned.

Miss Marsh had a funny feeling about this, but couldn't figure out what caused it. As she was walking around in the classroom teaching from her book, she noticed that Peter's head was bleeding. She asked him what happened, but he refused to tell her. Miss Marsh sent him to the school nurse but suspected something was happening in the boys' bathroom.

Even though she didn't belong in the boys' bathroom, she stormed in anyway. Just as she swung the door open, an older boy jumped out at her with his fists up. Upon seeing Miss Marsh, he panicked and jumped backward.

"What is going on?" she demanded. The frightened boy then admitted that this was an "initiation" into junior high school. Miss Marsh took action. The boy and Miss Marsh went to the principal. Then the matter was discussed between the boys of both grades and an end was put to this immature practice.

Try to keep in mind that violence of any sort cannot be tolerated and there are occasions when students shouldn't remain silent. These incidents need to be reported to the authorities. There is no shame in that.

Confidence isn't arrogance. It depends upon your opinion of yourself. It doesn't depend upon what others think of you. In Chapter 2, you listed some of your qualities. In the prior chapter, you noticed that you, as a teen, may misinterpret the actions of others and assume that they're rejections. You're going through a sensitive time of your life, but it's crucial that you reframe your thinking. Others aren't spending a lot of time thinking about you. They're thinking about—guess who?—themselves!

What About Those Who Don't Associate with Me?

A wise 14th century monk, John Lydgate, once said: "You can please some of the people all of the time, you can please all of the people some of the time, but you can't please all the people all the time." Presidents, Prime Ministers, billionaires, famous actors, and popular singers aren't liked by all of the people all of the time. It's not logical to feel that you're the curious exception to that. Others may dislike you because you have the same color hair that someone they dislike has! You don't need to take that personally. People have different personalities, and some are different from you. There is nothing wrong with that. They are entitled to their own personality and are accustomed to their own way of doing things. You can simply treat them courteously, as everybody deserves that. It's unhealthy to imagine that you can control their thoughts. Your focus should be about who you are, and it is you who wants to reach your fullest potential when you become an adult.

They're Not the Enemy!

What if you go to a social event or a party and you only know one other person, although not that well? What if you don't know anyone there? Then what do you do?

Easy peasy... Look around the room. Guaranteed, you'll notice someone who looks receptive and pleasant. They may even be sitting by themselves. Introduce yourself, and admit that you're a tad nervous because you don't know anyone there. If the other feels uncomfortable, they might say, "Oh, I feel the same way." You have now met a new friend. If the other knows some other people, she or he might introduce you. To boost your self-confidence, speak up and ask him or her to introduce you.

As you look around the room, notice the people. Is there anyone there whom you can complement on their attire? Is there a guy there with a team sweatshirt on? You can ask him about his school and team. Ask questions. Does he live nearby? Awaken your curiosity and try to find out something about the other guys, too. Let them do the talking and encourage them to continue. Find out their interests. That's a sign of self-confidence and maturity. What's more, your level of anxiety will drop.

What if You're Not Good Looking?

TV and the Internet are loaded with videos and photos of teens that meet some kind of imaginary standard set by the "they's" of the world—muscular guys, jocks, football players, and for the girls, these emaciated young women with waists that look like they're two inches wide! Gymnasts are often featured, and you can get their exercise programs via a streaming service. Other young women have tremendous sets of breasts, and they look top-heavy.

True Story: Sylvia

Sylvia, a 17-year-old, yearned for huge breasts, so she pleaded and pleaded with her parents to have her breasts enhanced. Finally, they gave in to her and when she was eighteen, they took her to a surgeon for a "boob job." It was difficult for her to handle at first, due to some medical issues, but she got it straightened out. She was very trim and was 5'4" high. After her surgery, she had size D breasts. That made her very popular with the guys, and she was

---

delighted. Sylvia got a lot of dates until she started going steady. However, in time, she started to develop pain in her back. It became more and more severe. Finally, a new doctor she went to delivered the bad news. He said the size of her breasts was putting a strain on her back. She had two options, he said, 1) wear a special brace that would relieve the pressure on her back, or 2) get a breast reduction.

Sylvia was horrified! If she wore the brace, she couldn't wear it with her bikini or even a two-piece bathing suit. She decided upon the brace, but took it off when she went swimming. Sylvia was like a bathing beauty, so she didn't wear her brace at the shore. Of course, she was in pain every time she went to the beach.

In time, Sylvia worked on building up her self-confidence and decided to be herself once again. So, she eventually had the breast reduction and made jokes when people commented about the change. The reverse surgery did resolve her physical problem, and she was delighted just being herself. However, she and her parents had needlessly spent thousands of dollars so she could learn that lesson.

Models go on starvation diets to model clothing. Some of them develop *Anorexia nervosa,* a severe eating disorder by which a person keeps eating less and less until they become too weak to model. Other models have been known to develop *Bulimia*. *Bulimia* is the practice of eating, enjoying the food, and then forcing themselves to vomit.

We were all born with our bodies. Perhaps some of you need diets, but being overweight doesn't mean anything bad about your personality, your qualities, or your values. Who you are isn't read on a scale. If you're self-conscious about the size of your nose, look around you. Look at everyone else's noses. There are plenty of big noses and crooked noses around!

Act with Trust in Yourself

The word "confidence" comes from the Latin word meaning "trust." Confidence means trust, and self-confidence means trust in yourself. Because you're outside of your comfort zone, you won't feel as certain about what you're about to do. If you dreamed about writing a novel, start it. You won't fly into it like a professional writer would, but the professional novelist, too, had to start without being sure it would work out.

Perhaps Jayne was worried about her relationship with her boyfriend. She wasn't sure or not if they were still going steady. Mike hadn't texted or called her recently. She sat down

72

for a while, took a few deep breaths, and relaxed in a lazy chair, composing what she would say. Then she approached Mike, with some trepidation, and talked about their issue.

Assertiveness

As you become an older teen, it sometimes becomes necessary to speak up for yourself. If a friend wants you to cut class with him and go to the mall, you need to think for yourself. Do you want to please your friend to the point that you'll let him or her talk you into it, or do you want to make up your own mind? You do have the skill to be polite and tell your friend you'd rather not go. Of course, you can tell the other person that they're free to go if they wish. That sort of dialog will make people respect you because it's mature.

On some occasions, though, a friend might say they're not going to talk to you anymore if you don't go along. Then they're acting a little like a bully, and you're jammed because your decision might cost you a friendship. Fortunately, some who threaten you with a break in your friendship may reconsider it later on. As a teen, you're on your way to adulthood and responsibilities. It is a difficult time, because there will be challenges like this where you need to make your own choices known. That takes courage and carries the obligation to be assertive and stand up for yourself no matter what.

Here is a story that tells the tale of what can happen if you don't abide by your own more mature choices. It tells of consequences:

Wandering Around in New York

Leslie and Jennifer always traveled to school together on the same bus. One day, Jennifer wanted to stay on the bus, which also went to New York City. She wanted to go backstage at one of the theaters to meet her favorite rock star who was scheduled to appear on stage. She begged her friend, Leslie, to go with her. Leslie knew they were both supposed to go to school. However, the invitation was tempting, and Jennifer said she wouldn't talk to Leslie anymore if she didn't take off school that day.

Leslie wasn't assertive, as she didn't want to lose Jennifer as a friend. So, the two of them stayed on the bus. An hour later, the bus pulled into Port Authority Terminal, and the two girls exited. Fortunately, Leslie had enough cash with her, so they could find their way to the theater.

They popped out of the terminal, hailed a cab, and had the driver take them to the theater. They were excited and took some time to wander around, enjoying the sights and sounds of the great city.

They walked to the theater, but the ticket booth wasn't open. Then Jennifer noticed a door next to the box office. It had sign on it saying, "Employees only." Nothing else.

"This must be the side door into the theater," said Jennifer happily. Sure enough, it was unlocked and the two girls entered. The place had changing rooms with some names on them. The two girls were exploding with excitement.

All the changing rooms were empty! As they strolled up the hallways, they saw cosmetics on the dressing tables. Still, no one was there.

Suddenly, they heard a noise and ran toward it. At the end of one of the hallways, a janitor was mopping the floor. No one else was in sight, and they kept looking in all the empty rooms.

The two girls then interrupted the janitor. He looked up in surprise. Then Leslie asked him where the rock star was. He looked at the two girls as if he thought they were crazy. He answered them solemnly, "He's not here. The rock stars don't arrive until much later, in time for their shows. They come in their own trailers."

The two girls were shocked. It was only 11 AM! For hours, they wandered about until they finally came to their senses and took a bus home.

Jennifer went to her house, and Leslie walked a couple of blocks to her house. Leslie lied to her parents and said that school was dismissed early.

That didn't work, as the principal had called her parents, asking why Leslie wasn't at class. Uh oh! Her parents were furious and explained to her that she and Jennifer might have been attacked by thugs on the streets.

Leslie hadn't thought about that, and realized that the two of them could have been in danger. Her parents then grounded her for a week and she had to go to detention at school.

Those were the consequences of not being assertive.

It takes confidence and assertiveness to stand up for yourself and do what's right as Leslie discovered the hard way. Challenge yourself to make your preferences known to others.

Practice stating your preferences, and refrain from indecisiveness. You know what is best, and now it's time to stand up for yourself. Others will occasionally try to persuade you to do things their way, even when they're not good for you. Some might want you to experiment with strange drugs, go get drunk, or smoke.

What are your values? What are your beliefs? What are your principles? It's OK to ask an older person when you're confused or suspect you'll get into trouble if you're presented with something questionable.

Drinking and Drugs

Suppose you're at a gathering, and people are trying to pressure you into taking some kind of unknown drug. They'll tell you, "It'll make you feel good." What they won't tell you is the fact that you may get hooked on it. You might try the drug, but the first time is the most dangerous, because you will like it. Drugs can cost you money and build up insane urges in you. They can make you desperate for more. That is the nature of addiction.

Drugs also have side effects. Initially, they may not be of concern to you, but—in time—can cause you to become non-functional.

True Story: Carol's Upside-Down Event

One day, Larry tempted his girlfriend, Carol, to try out a drug. He didn't tell her what it was. Instead of refusing it, she permitted herself to be persuaded and popped the pill in her mouth.

It felt terrific...at first. She was very relaxed and happy. THEN...suddenly she started hearing things a minute after they were spoken. Then she saw Larry sitting on the couch, and then—in shock—she saw him sit on the couch again! Movements he made repeated themselves. Then he looked like he was upside-down!

Carol lay down in a bed, and images were swirling around and around in her mind. She was hallucinating. Larry was no help, as he was caught up inside his own upside-down mind.

Finally, Carol fell asleep. When she awoke, she was woozy, but gratefully nothing was upside-down. Then Carol realized that she was supposed to take her brother to the park. Larry was sound asleep and was too debilitated to take her home.

Carol wasn't assertive because she could have refused the drug, but she realized that she needed help and called her father.

Later she and her parents discussed the event and Carol was honest about it. Her parents were most compassionate. Carol broke off her relationship with Larry—a wise decision. Her parents didn't punish her, as they (and she) realized that she learned a lesson the hard way.

Drugs, Alcohol, and Anxiety

You may have tried out some drugs and alcohol. Guess what, though! If you ever got drunk, you probably felt great— as in r-e-l-a-x-e-d.

You may have also noticed schoolmates who've gotten drunk or strung out on drugs are wasted most of the time. This is something they use to escape their feelings of stress and anxiety. So, what's the big deal?

The big deal is this—the very first drug…the very first drinking binge…leads to others. They say you'll get addicted, but you think you can control it. *Well, you can't!* It's controlled by your body. There are pleasure hormones your body produces now and again—serotonin, epinephrine, cortisol, and dopamine. (*Dopamine*—what an appropriate name!) Drugs and alcohol make your body produce more of those hormones artificially. You've seen what drugs and alcohol has done to some kids. In a few years, they lose their ambition to succeed in life. That's very sad. You've also heard tragic stories about singers and actors who took a tad too much. And now they're gone—right at the height of their careers. They thought they could control it too, but they were wrong. Their love of the drugs and alcohol won out over their common sense.

It is very, very hard sometimes to resist the temptation of taking drugs and drinking beer. But—remember—the first time is the most dangerous. So it's important you learn all the tricks to avoid wasting away your life, and develop other interests instead and find out all your strengths and the beauty that is you before it's too late.

Social groups and parties you go to may present you with other choices. Sometimes, the kids at the party might want you to try a drink. Of course, it is against the law for underage teens to imbibe alcohol. If you have practiced making wise and mature choices, those occasions may arise. When they are persistent, that is your opportunity to resist them. That is the time to be assertive. You might say something like, "If you continue to try to get me to drink, I will have to leave." You need all the might of your courage, as you are again faced with the dilemma of risking friendships and making a mature decision for yourself. The others are violating you by insisting that you engage in something that conflicts with your values. You may have to set boundaries for such friends who are less mature than you are. Everywhere you go in life, it is occasionally necessary to help others respect you and your own boundaries. Some activities are unacceptable to you. Assertiveness calls for you to remind people of those boundaries.

When you say "No," it doesn't mean you're being selfish. It is self-love. Self-love is natural and healthy. Others not only will respect you for being your own person, but you will be able to make new friends who are more like you, and who hold the same values and principles you have. Like you, they don't drink or take drugs. Your new group is more mature and all of you can have interesting and forward-looking relationships. All of you are preparing for college, vocational schools, and careers. All of you have decisions to make that will shape your future lives and allow you to reach your full potential.

So, be brave; be assertive and embark on a journey to discover who you will become in the world of tomorrow.

Chapter 5 – Up and Down: Emotional Control

True Story: Great Uncle Tim

Melanie planned on going to Pam's house one Saturday afternoon. All the girls would be there, and they were going to experiment with different hair styles. That morning, Mrs. Fielding announced that Great Uncle Tim was coming so she and her little brother, Jon-Jon, had to be there to visit with him.

"OH, NO!" Melanie shrieked. "I'M NOT STAYING HOME THIS AFTERNOON!"

Melanie argued and argued with her mother. It wasn't fair, she thought, as she only had the weekends to spend with her friends. Finally, Melanie's mother gave her that angry stare, so Melanie thought better of it and stomped off. She'd "fix" her mother. She decided she wouldn't talk to anybody when her uncle came!

It nearly happened that way, too. Melanie only gave her uncle one or two-word answers. She just sat on the old hassock and pouted. Her little brother made up for it, though, by chattering away like he usually did.

After the visit, Mrs. Fielding went outside to water the flowers. Melanie and her brother went outside. Then he asked their mother for some cookies and soda. He was overweight and was on a diet, so she turned him down. Jon-Jon threw a tantrum. He hollered and threw himself on the ground kicking and screaming bloody murder. It was loud enough for the neighbors to hear. Suddenly, Jon-Jon's mother turned the hose toward him. *WOW!* He got sprayed in the face! He was OK, because the spray was a gentle one, but he stopped. He really stopped. It was the shock he needed to change his horrible mood. Jon-Jon then realized what he'd done. He was afraid someone saw him, and went inside without a word.

Once Melanie got inside, she went to her room. Suddenly, she remembered something—she had done practically the same thing as little Jon-Jon. She, too, threw a tantrum about Uncle Tim's visit!

> Melanie was embarrassed, as Jon-Jon was eight-years-old, and she was all of fifteen! Although she didn't throw herself on the ground, she shouldn't have lost her temper. Great Uncle Tim didn't come over that often, and he was always nice. Melanie's friend, Pam, was much more mature and wouldn't do such a thing, Melanie thought.

Why did Melanie's emotions go crazy like that? Why did she swing from anger to pouting? She was at the stage of deciding colleges soon, and she wanted to be a veterinarian. Melanie thought only of her disappointment instead of considering a mature reaction when her plans changed. She later realized that she hadn't acted her age.

Emotional Control: Stop and Think

You, as a teen, are on the path to adulthood, even though you may think of yourself as that already. It is time to become aware of your feelings, labeling them for what they are, why they happen, and assuming responsibility for them. The teen years are a tender time, and a time to develop awareness of the reactions that others have may have if you say or behave badly. Others have emotional reactions, and it's important not to hurt their feelings. Kindness and courtesy are appreciated by others, even one's parents. It's not a time when you can profit from separating your intelligent mind from your feelings. It's what separates humans from the animals.

The teen years are turbulent times in many ways. Adolescents are in the process of putting aside their childish ways, and yet haven't developed all the social skills of adults. Also, this is a time of self-discovery. Teens only have a whisper of an idea about what kind of traits they will exhibit as an adult. No two people are the same, and no two teenagers are the same. This time of one's life will determine one's future.

Thoughts are okay and fine, but expression of the nice and nasty feelings that follow thoughts must be monitored. Sometimes, "thought-changing" is called for, when one's thoughts are dragging them down. There will be occasions when you come precariously close to losing your temper, and be tempted to say things that are better left unsaid. You can risk losing friends if you permit yourself to start hollering at them. Learning to think before you speak is the first phase of emotional control. Emotional control can lead to happier and healthier relationships.

Root Causes

It's vital to analyze the *real* cause of a feeling you're experiencing. Perhaps it's because you're jealous of the other person. Maybe it's because they're not doing something the way you want it done. And—unfortunate but true—the other person may be acting "mean." Why? Perhaps you're being bossy, "hyper," angry, sad, or just don't feel well.

You may even be excluded from an activity that your friends plan on doing. Try to figure out the *real reason* you're feeling bad. What are the facts of the case? If you still feel the other person is at fault, plan on turning a complaint into a request. For example, if your friends are going to the store and they didn't invite you to come along, plan on saying, "I feel bad you didn't invite me along to go shopping. May I come with you?" It's less offensive than saying, "You guys are mean! You didn't invite me to the store!" Doesn't that first choice sound better? People don't respond well to criticism. After all, they may have overlooked you accidentally and will apologize. That way you won't lose any friendships, and others will respect you for being mature. The real root causes for your emotional reactions may be very different from what you imagined. This is the second phase of emotional control.

Resolution

You secretly want others to do things the way you'd like them done. That isn't realistic. Others will differ with you on various issues. This presents a difficulty. You and the other person now need to discuss the problem in such a way that it shows respect for each other. It may be difficult to hear the other if they say something you don't like, but control will take care of that if you continue to hold back a wild emotional reaction. Then, and only then, can you and your friend solve the problem. This is the third and last phase of emotional control.

Steps:

Review the steps involved in achieving emotional control:

- Stop and Think
  This is the first phase of emotional control. It entails stopping and thinking about the problematic issue first before you react, lest you respond angrily or start hollering (or crying).

- Root Causes
  Try to look inward and figure out the real reason you're upset. When you complete doing this, you may realize that the real reason is different from what you first thought it was.

- Resolution

  Although you now know the real reason for being upset, this is the hardest phase of emotional control. This is when you discuss the issue with the other person. Trying to be calm is difficult, and talking about it maturely is likewise difficult.

  There is a reward in resolving a situation with emotional control. You will feel closer to the other person or at least come to an understanding that will leave both of you feeling at peace with yourselves.

Learning how to calm yourself is an important way to gain a sense of emotional control. You need a break from the barrage that your schoolmates and society itself brings you. Now that you're nearly an adult, those demands will increase, so it's good to have a zone of escape.

Meditation is becoming quite trendy, and the teenage years are a perfect time to start. It's not a religious practice. It's a practice that helps people quiet the "noisy" mind that's trying to sucker you into worry, anxiety, and stress. You have needs too. You deserve to feel good about yourself. Loving yourself is an instinct that all of you have. You are entitled to it. It also helps you become much, much calmer, and you won't lose your temper nor experience the "jitters" when confronted with an exam or interact with a troublesome classmate.

Mindfulness meditation techniques are very, very simple. It takes no study. It only requires that you have a time by yourself without interruptions. People who've established a schedule that contains meditations have reported that the meditations bring them a calmness and serenity others don't enjoy. Each meditation can be merely fifteen minutes each. Most successful meditators set up a certain time of day to practice their meditations. Once you start with a schedule, don't eliminate them. Otherwise you'll get out of the habit of doing it.

Mindfulness Meditation Exercise #1

This practice is a technique that originated in Buddhism. It has been modified into a Western version that suits people who live here. It's ideal for calming the nerves. Who's ever seen a Buddhist monk losing his temper? No one. This meditation is a simple breathing exercise that will restore to a state of feeling okay with yourself and with others.

1. Relax in a comfortable chair with the lights turned down low or the blinds closed. Breathe slowly and rhythmically. Breathe through your nose and exhale through your mouth. Accept the fact that you're

having intruding thoughts, but just let them go without thinking much about them.

2. Concentrate on relaxing your head. You'll feel comfortable if you bow your head a little and close your eyes partially. Be sure to keep on breathing slowly. The thoughts will come back again, but patiently let them pass by. You may not succeed entirely, so try not to think deeply about them. They'll soon leave.

3. Relax your neck and your upper body. Again, focus on your breathing. It will distract you from wandering back into interrupting thoughts.

4. Relax your arms and legs. Keep breathing rhythmically. Stay there for a while, listening to your breathing.

5. Slowly, ever so slowly, start feeling more energy pouring into your body, like a light coming into your head.

6. Imagine the light getting brighter and brighter. Then stand up slowly.

You're at peace with yourself. You're proud of who you are, and you're grateful for your friends and family and all people who make your life brighter.

The other aspect that will help you is to schedule a time and place to practice mindfulness meditations. The ideal session for a mindfulness meditation is thirty minutes. However, if you can only afford to spare fifteen minutes, do it. These meditations can be life-savers. Those who've engaged in them have reported that they have become less stressed-out and don't get hung up on the little things.

Mindfulness Meditation Exercise #2

Mindfulness meditations are more interesting if you go outside on summer nights when you can. Select nights when the stars are in the sky.

1. Lie down in a lawn chair and marvel at the wonders of the sky. Inhale the night air deeply. Breathe in through the nose and exhale through the mouth. Work on doing this rhythmically.

2. Thoughts will intrude. Just let them come, but don't dwell on any one of them. Simply let them drift in and out, without your partaking of them.

3. Return to focusing upon your rhythmic breathing every time your mind wanders. Ignore the sounds of cars and even the crickets. Just let them pass. Your focus is on the universe above you- the wonders of a dark sky that stretches on into forever.

4. Continue your breathing routine, and become aware that the universe is entering into you and

encompassing your body. You are one with the universe and the universe is one with you. Feel the life of being.

5. Breathe a little while longer, until you are ready to leave. You will miss being there, but will carry it with you for the rest of the night and into the next day. It will bring you a peace society cannot.

Chapter 6 – Money, and Sports

At this point in life, you as a teen are preparing to manage your finances. Imagine that! You've been looking forward to becoming an adult, but now comes the time when your parents won't just give you all the money you need. It's time for you to take some responsibility paying your way and preparing to become a full-time contributor to society.

Every family organizes money matters differently. Sometimes teens may not have a job yet, and their parents will have to determine how much money to give their teens to take care of some expenses. Perhaps, you will have an allowance to cover school expenses, lunches, snacks, clothing, and electronic devices like cell phones and a computer tablet. Maybe you'll be able to get a job and earn your own money at least part-time during the summer and on weekends.

When a teen like you is in the house, parents may ask that you contribute to household duties. For years they have been taking care of your laundry and your meals. They will ask you to help with tasks like preparing some meals, mowing the lawn, gardening, taking out the garbage, cleaning the house, and walking and feeding the dog. If you have very young brothers or sisters, you may be asked to help out with them. You will also have more social activities, and that means that you will have to change your clothes more frequently to get ready for work or an outing with your friends. You have a set of "school clothes," and a set of clothes you wear when you visit your friends. In keeping with the trends, they're hardly ever the same.

The Meeting

Your parents will want to sit down with you and make financial decisions. First of all, you'll need a bank account, a credit or debit card, and CASH. Listen to your parents' advice on the banking and credit card issue. They've had their ups and downs with interest rates and banking—they get it. Here's a learning experience Matt had:

True Story: Stuck for Hours

Matt decided to go out with some of the guys. One of them drove Matt and the other two guys on a one-hour trip. They went to the amusement park and the animal park. Of course, they had their hot dogs—plenty of them! They bought food for the animals and the tickets for the rides. They had a great

---

time.

At the end of the day, the driver dropped off two of the boys, but announced he wouldn't be able to drive Matt all the way home because Matt lived in the other direction. The driver was going to go to his uncle's house which was near the animal park. What a surprise!

Matt's friend dropped him off in a nearby town, so Matt could take a cab home. Yes, it would be a lot of money, but he had no choice. When he walked up to the taxi stand, he stopped dead in his tracks. Matt only had his credit cards, and the taxi only took cash! Uh oh!

He was stuck having to call Mom and Dad to ask for help. He couldn't believe he did this. They were both annoyed because he was an hour away. That meant that one or the other parent would have to drive one hour up to pick up Matt, then turn around and drive for another hour to get home.

The moral of the story is to always have sufficient cash on you...not so much that you could be robbed, but enough to survive and make your own way home.

The first responsibility you and your parents have is to create a budget. Decide how much you need to take to school for food and other educational expenses, how much you need for transportation, like buses, and how much for fun stuff like snacks and soft drinks. You have to account for your needs in terms of paying for your phone time. That's something you should do from your allowance. There are other devices and software you might need along with apps you might want. *Beware!* If you haven't had the annoying experience of being charged for even small phone activities, you may be charged a lot. Be wise in selecting what you really need, and be frugal. Some of your Internet apps call for subscriptions. Take out your pen and work out what services and equipment you really want and those you don't need. Do this ahead of time to avoid rash decisions. It isn't meant as an insult if your parents warn you about the deviousness of advertisers. They and you don't want to be manipulated into a purchase that's going to blossom into a huge expense. It's very trendy to buy the latest smartphone. New ones are more expensive. You may have to resist peer pressure to turn away from the temptation to buy new models yearly.

Clothes and social expenses are costly. Parents and you as the teen need to budget what should be used for those as well. These items can get to be too high if you don't watch:

1. Designer and trendy clothes

2. SNEAKERS ($$$$!)

3. Cosmetics

4. Dances and the school prom (very, very expensive if you go)

5. Spring Break? Most parents will allow their teens to go, but you must be careful if you're going to another country or hang out with people you don't know. They may be responsible, but there's no guarantee. You should always associate with the foreigners in groups of people you know and trust.

Some of the kids will bring alcohol with them. If you aren't of drinking age, this will present a problem for you, as you will be coaxed and coaxed to drink. Hang out with other non-drinkers from your class. Your self-control will be severely tested.

Giving in to pressure from other kids can have consequences you may not like. It will be embarrassing if you get drunk, and no one is going to want to be saddled with a person who can't stand without wobbling and who says embarrassing things at the top of their lungs!

Remember this, too—if you have some part-time work you can get paid for, it might be better to skip the spring break. You can save up a bundle of money because employers will need help during that time. There will be lots of time to make up for that week in your life when you can have fun at the beach or wherever you're going.

6. Concerts

There will be opportunities for rock concerts. They're wild; they're fun and loud. One thing all of them have in common is the fact they're expensive, especially the mosh pits. Most likely, the mosh pits will break your budget.

7. Cars

If you're of driving age, your parents may want to buy you a reliable older car. You will want the latest hot models around—an SUV, sports model, or a truck. This can create a problem with your parents because of the expense.

This also is a time you need to be honest with yourself. Some teens drive safely, but unfortunately, there are others among you who don't. Be honest and choose wisely when selecting a vehicle.

8. Dates

    You guys should be careful in terms of arranging dates. If you plan on going to the movies and then to dinner afterward, a sit-down dinner can be costly. If that's what you want to do, it would be wise to stop by the restaurant ahead of time and check out their menu for prices. You certainly don't want to be embarrassed if you don't have enough money in the bank to cover your debit card, or go beyond your limit on your credit card. A cash tip is usually nicer than adding it to the restaurant bill. It makes a good impression on your date if you know what you're doing.

9. Online Spending

    As a young man or lady, you will most likely have the freedom to buy online. Most things are inexpensive, but you must take care not to overspend. That's easy to do, and you might end up with a hefty overdraft fee at the bank, or they might turn down your purchase halfway through the transaction! Then you have to click your way out of trouble. You may even have to borrow from your friends or parents. And you *know* how your parents will react to that!

10. Sports or Cheerleading

Most sports in which you will participate have expenses involved. You may have to buy your uniform and pay fees related to the sport.

Speaking of Sports

Plan ahead:

If you have to try out first to join a sport, it's best to approach a few experienced players first. Learn what you can from them in terms of playing the sport and find out about the procedures to be followed. Francie didn't do that. She wanted to join the cheerleading squad but didn't seek any advice from the other cheerleaders in advance:

Francie: The Wannabe Cheerleader

During the summer right before Francie was eligible to become a cheerleader, she failed to ask some of the other girls about it. When try-outs came in September, she and the other hopefuls went out on the field. First of all, four girls demonstrated a routine they had rehearsed during the summer. They did cartwheels, stood on their hands in

---

unison, and called out a cheer they learned. Then they did a few flips.

The next few girls went out on to the field. They did somersaults, cartwheels, and back flips. Francie stood on the side and watched in terror. All she could do was a cartwheel, and didn't even do it that well.

As might be expected, most of the girls were placed on the team, but Francie and one other girl—Maureen—were rejected.

Francie was upset, and so was Maureen, as a matter of fact. Francie cried, but just a little. She gained emotional control and thought about it first. Then she realized she made an error and gave into her shyness. That was the root cause for her failure. She took responsibility for it.

Then she looked at poor Maureen who was moping near the fence. Francie then realized that the two of them had the same experience and this could help them become friends. Afterward, Maureen and Francie became terrific friends. They linked up with another girl, Carolyn. Their parents then invited the girls over to each other's houses, and even dropped them off at the movies and ice cream store once in a while.

It so happened that all three girls became very close friends. They even went to the same college together and kept in touch after that.

At the Games:

Your parents will want to attend your high school games. Most parents are very encouraging and will help you feel better if you don't perform well. However, your parents, too, used to play sports when they went to high school and college. Some parents may pressure you into playing their favorite sport. You may or may not want to. Here is an instance when you will have to exercise your emotional control and stand up for yourself, but do it respectfully. In the prior chapter, there was some advice as to how to handle disagreements with your friends. You may have to handle disagreements with your parents as well. Use some of those same techniques.

Perhaps you're not the best player at your chosen sport, but your Dad keeps pushing you to perform better. It's not unusual for a parent to come storming out on your field and engage in a loud argument with your coach over how he or she is handling your position in the game. Perhaps your coach might want you to sit out a certain segment of the game, and your dad disagrees with him. Now what?

You know your parents aren't perfect either. Everyone makes mistakes that can cause embarrassment. This is a time for silence on your part. This is a time for you to withdraw from the situation and let the adults handle it. If either one of them asks you questions, respond with respect, and be honest. Play it delicately, and play it "safe."

Chapter 7 – Your First Jobs

You probably thought this chapter should be called "Your First Job," not "Jobs." Many teens have problems with their very first job. The first job you get is going to be a tad traumatic, although you may shrug it off as easy. It's a whole new world out there, and it doesn't operate like school or college.

There are different procedures used by various companies. *Totally different!* Don't make the mistake of assuming that a simple job at a delicatessen is casual. It all depends. Research the company ahead of time. Even if it's as basic as a grocery store, you might try talking to a few employees first, just to get an idea. Companies have web sites, and those will also give you a lot of information.

Initial Procedure: Some jobs require that you apply online on a rather extensive application. They may want you to do a Zoom or Skype interview. No matter what, have a resume ready, and present it along with your written application. It will show your seriousness and interest. Some job interviews are more casual, but be prepared for anything.

Practice interviewing by asking a friend to role-play one with you. Ask a few people—preferably older ones, who aren't your parents—to provide references for you. Asking teachers and coaches for references can be a great place to start. Have a few questions prepared to ask the interviewer. It will show that you truly have interest. Before you enter the room to be interviewed, turn your cell phone off.

Even if the employees there wear jeans and other casual clothing, you should go in something a little nicer. Again, it depends upon the kind of job you've applied to.

There will be a LOT of applicants. Some companies have so many that they go through the applications and resumes they have first, and select the top group they might like to choose from. It's an unnerving experience, but try to relax.

Procedure: Always look at the interviewer directly. They'll want to know *why* you want to work for them (as opposed to someone else). Never say, "Because I need the money." Employers want to feel that you deliberately chose their company. In some of your responses, try to include some of the things you've learned about the company. It will show that you're not only prepared, but you're a serious and diligent person. Think about what skills you already have that will be an asset to the company. The interviewer will ask you a little bit about yourself. Prepare for that. Don't rub your body or touch your face. You can present yourself well at an interview. You've had so much practice in school—imagine that a new teacher just entered your classroom.

Make a few notes (not too many) on a small notepad. Thank the interviewer at the end and ask when you might hear whether or not you're hired. Call or email them on that day to say thank you for the interview. It could be that the employer is trying to decide between you and another person. That phone call or email might land you the job!

True Story: The Shipping Company

In a small Eastern town, the interviewer held a group interview. Most of the candidates looked quite decent. They were neither overdressed nor underdressed, except for one guy who had on ripped and dirty jeans. At the interview table there were two female candidates who, no doubt, would have been rejected immediately. One girl was ambitiously filing her nails as the interviewer entered the room, and checking her makeup in a small mirror. Another girl had fingernails that were nearly five inches long!

So, your general appearance is important, but it's a time that you need to look and act traditionally. Employers generally don't want anyone who's sloppy or who's more interested in their appearance than in their jobs.

While it might seem silly to make those obvious errors, they do happen.

Common Mistakes

Be sure you're familiar with the employee handbook you'll be given when you're hired. Your first job will be *nothing* like school. Your supervisor will tell you to do things, some of which make absolutely no sense to you. Yes, it's true! In your head, you may be able to think of far more efficient ways of performing those tasks. Remember this—there are reasons that certain tasks are done in ways you don't agree with, but you may not know those reasons. If you did, then it would make perfect sense to you, but no one has the time to explain all that to you.

You won't like all the tasks assigned to you. Of course, do them anyway as long as they are not illegal or harmful to you. Supervisors and even employees in other departments may instruct you to do tasks for them. Be careful! Because you're new, you may not know whether you're supposed to do that other work or not, so ask your direct supervisor. Some employees may be testing you to see if you'll do their work for them, too. Never pretend you understand something if you don't. Find out which fellow employees you can trust and ask them pertinent questions. This is called office politics. It's difficult to learn and troublesome to navigate.

Keep in mind that you've been hired because the company felt you would be valuable to them. Return that vote of confidence by recognizing the fact that you represent the company, and their goals are your goals. You aren't just simply "doing a job;" you want *your* company to succeed and be profitable. After all, if it didn't, neither would you! Avoid criticizing anyone there. In certain cases, that may be hard to do. Try not to associate with other employees who are very negative and critical of the company. They will try to suck you into their way of thinking and make you unhappy there.

True Story: The Banging End

Emil just got a job at a printing company. He worked in a computer stall along with many other people. He was busily involved in preparing invoices for the company's customers. Emil was totally involved in doing his work correctly, as he applied careful attention to it.

Five o'clock marked the end of the workday there, except for the print shop in the back. Suddenly, at 4:45, Emil heard loud banging. He quickly sat up straight and turned his head all around. What was going on? Then he noticed that every single employee was putting all their work away, gathering up their things, shutting drawers, and hustling around the room.

Then they sat back impatiently and stared at the clock! The

---

very second it was five o'clock, *all* of them leaped up, pushed their chairs in loudly, and nearly ran out of the door!

From his seat, Emil heard all the cars start up with a thunderous roar. Through the window, he could see all the cars compete to be the first one out! Then the lot was nearly empty except for the supervisors' car, the boss's car, and Emil's car.

The employees, of course, were anxious to get home. This work behavior doesn't make a good impression. Those who try to finish up the last segment of their work demonstrate an interest in the quality of their work. In many ways, your work is an important part of who you are as a person. If, in the future, the company has to make layoffs, you may keep your job, as you showed that you were diligent. What's more, you might even get a raise or promotion!

Come in on time every day, or slightly earlier, and don't leave in the giant hurry described above.

Stress at Work

You, as a teen, will have some stress, and your first job can possibly be a traumatic experience. As stated earlier, work is *nothing* like school. Also mentioned earlier, office politics are tricky to manage. It's not unlike those former classmates of yours who covered the range of personalities you have to deal with. It may be challenging, though, as many of them have so much more experience than you have.

Many of the employees may be bossy. Some people are impertinent and will try to give you some of their work. In moderation, of course, you should be of help, but not to the extent that you're overtaxed. And—wait—many of your colleagues will give you lots and lots of advice. Find a trusted friend who is diligent and courteous. That person may help you ride the wild waves of office politics. You know what's going on, but the real question is—what's *really* going on?

Try not to be too flippant or casual at work. Swearing is a "no-no," and sensitive co-workers and your supervisors won't like it. Professionalism and courtesy are the best courses to follow.

At your new job, it's wise to make an appointment with your supervisor early on. Ask him or her how you are doing. Is your work satisfactory? Again, this will show true interest in the quality of your work and says a lot of positive things about you as a person.

The City Planner

Emil's second job was with a surveyor. He assisted the chief surveyor in measuring properties. Eventually, his employer taught him how to handle some of the paperwork for the municipality for whom the surveyor worked. He really liked it and learned more and more throughout the two summers he worked for the man.

When he entered college, Emil knew what he wanted as a major and got an undergraduate degree in Urban Planning from a state university. After graduation, he was able to qualify for very lucrative positions in his own state and across the country. Your temporary and part-time jobs will help you gain precious experience and may even become a career.

The Curse of the Job-Hoppers

Perhaps your first job is a temporary summer job or short-lived. That's OK, but now you have some job experience—a fact that will serve you well when you apply for another job. It's quite common to dislike your first job. If it's not a temporary or summer job, try to hang in there for at least a year. When you apply for a new job, it doesn't speak well for you if you can't last at a job for at least a year.

Fortunately, most companies realize that you're adapting to a whole new world "out there." They won't lapse into shock if you want to move on. Just a suggestion, though—don't quit without having another job lined up. You may run out of spending money, and your parents won't want to start paying your way again. They're bound to be disappointed, too, if you don't have a new job lined up. Despite all that's happened between you and them at home, they're well-meaning and want the best for you. Deep down, they want you to do even better than they did when they were in their teens or early 20s. They'll be proud of you, even if you have a humble job like sweeping floors or flipping hamburgers.

For the first few jobs you have, keep all of this advice in mind. *AVOID "JOB-HOPPING!"* "Job-hopping" occurs when you jump from one job to another job to another job and so on. On work applications, as you know, they always ask for your job experience. It doesn't look well if you have many former jobs listed. You might consider stretching the times you've worked for other jobs, or condense the lists somehow.

114

Be ready for the magic question on the part of a future employer: "Why did you leave your former job?" Work out an answer that sounds reasonable, and don't speak ill of the former company or the former supervisors, regardless. Your interviewer may very well call one of your former employers, so keep that in mind when you tell him why you left your other job. If you came in late most days, they will definitely tell your new prospect that fact. If he's seriously considering you, he may ask your former employer, "Is so-and-so 'eligible for rehire?'" That's a "killer question."

These are good responses: "I saw your job advertised, and I really think it's a better match for my skills," or, "I'm familiar with your company and wanted to work for you before, but there weren't any openings when I applied." Be prepared for possible follow-up questions, and answer them as honestly as makes sense.

"Job-hoppers" can get away with that behavior for years. Unfortunately, they will find it difficult to rise in the ranks, and may even reach a point when no one will hire them. Some can be unemployed then for years.

If you work at a company long enough, you can get unemployment insurance, but it does run out. When you try to reapply, they may want you to show proof that you've been actively seeking work. In time, it gets more and more difficult, as you are young and employable.

You want to reach your full potential as a person. You want to feel good about yourself and proud of your accomplishments. Periods of unemployment can serve to throw you into depression, if you don't put a stop to it. You don't want to play games with the state, and it's not emotionally fulfilling to try to get the government to support you.

Chapter 8 – Hello? Hello?

Active Listening

Did you know that people spend about 55% of the day listening, but only really hear and remember about 17 to 25% of what is said?

Don't you hate it when you're talking to your friend, but she's so busy texting other people that she's not paying attention to you? Well, you don't want to do that to your close friends, either. If you ask your friends not to text while you're talking, they'll do it just to keep your friendship. Don't be afraid to tell your friend to turn her phone off for a little while. You are important, and they are important to you. Those texters are just "interrupters." They can leave messages, and there's no race to answer them right away. It's rude to interrupt two people who are having a face-to-face conversation. Besides, no one can listen successfully to two conversations at once.

When your friend, your parents, or your coach is talking to you, you'll avoid misunderstandings if you learn active listening skills. *Active* listening skills differ from casual listening. Everyone tends to think of their own responses before the speaker is even finished. Suppose your mother said she'd pick you up at your girlfriend's house and not the mall as usual. If you weren't listening properly you might be standing outside the mall wondering what happened to her. Then you and she would get into an argument. Who wants that? What happened? You let yourself get distracted.

Suppose someone has an issue with you and wants to discuss it. Perhaps they will start by saying something you don't like. If you interrupt, they may feel that you disrespected them, and you won't hear the full message. Of course, you didn't mean to disrespect them, but that's how it will come across to them. Let them finish. Then pause. Clarify their statement; for example, ask, "You don't want me to come over on Saturday? How come?" Now, you're giving them a chance to explain. Maybe it's because your friend may say he has to get ready for a date later on. Maybe his stepdad is going to be there then, and he knows he has to spend all his time with him. That might be a topic for the two of you to discuss. It will show that you care about your friend and are curious about his relationship with his stepdad. Showing you care will draw you closer to your friend.

There are ways to say things that won't be offensive. Suppose you didn't invite your friend over last Sunday, and your friend was hurt by that. Then suppose he says, "I can't believe you didn't invite me over last Sunday!" Your friend now put you on the defensive, but you can dodge that. Here's how—keep your voice deep and speak slowly. Ask, "Are you upset I didn't invite you over?" Then let's say he was. You can then explain why; for instance, you might say, "I had Earl and Margaret over, but you don't get along well with Earl, do you?" Or, if it was an oversight on your part, you might want to apologize. "Oh, I'm sorry. I was so busy that I just didn't think of it." Then you have the opportunity of setting up an alternate plan with your friend to make up for it. Remember to keep your voice calm.

The trick to wording this without offending anyone is to focus on the other person's feelings. Avoid interrupting. Listen to them very carefully and keep your mind open. Don't assume they're going to say anything offensive.

Become Popular at the Gathering

Suppose you're at a group event. The hosts or hostesses tend to introduce you very quickly to people you don't know. It's tough to remember all their names, but it's easy to remember just a few. Try associating a few of the names with a physical feature they have, and connect the name with that characteristic. For example:

Joe the Nose	Tracy the Curl
Matt the Giant	Amy the Round

Joe is the guy with the large nose; Matt has a Giants team sweatshirt on; Tracy has curly hair, and Amy has a round face (and maybe a round body too!). You're now equipped to approach any one of those new kids and address them by name. Dale Carnegie, a public speaking coach and business advisor, taught his classes that, "A person's name is to that person the sweetest, most important sound in any language." If you can pull this off, your listener will immediately like you. The next step is to get them (not you) to tell them about themselves. Ask them where they live. Then ask them something they don't expect like, "Do you like it there?" That's a loaded question. Everyone has all kinds of opinions about their hometown. You can follow up with questions like: "What do you do for fun?" Avoid dead-end questions like "What school do you go to?" Or any questions that will most likely have one-word answers.

In fact, you can spend some time at night preparing open-ended questions like those above. Try to ask follow-up questions to what others tell you. Be curious. When you look at people, try not to fidget or play with your hair. It's distracting. When you look at someone, look between their eyes at the bridge of their nose. To them, it will appear as if you're looking at both their eyes at once. It also gives the other the impression that you're really interested in them as a person. Nod when they go on for a while. When there's a pause, reflect on a feeling they might have about what they're saying. For example, "Oh, you must have been very excited when _____ happened." If it was a negative feeling they expressed, you might say, "Oh, that sounds like a real downer. Was it?"

Sometimes there are silences in a conversation. There's no need to rush in and fill that empty time with meaningless chatter. You can suggest you and your new friend go to the snack table. That's a comfortable break and gives the other person the opportunity to talk to someone else, if they wish.

Avoid "You" responses when someone says something you don't agree with or don't like. Instead of saying, "I can't believe *you* said that," change it to reflect *your* feelings and not theirs. Something like, "*I get the feeling* that you're annoyed with me. Are you?" Here, you're opening the door to honest discussion. You also paid the other person a compliment of sorts because you acknowledged the fact that they're entitled to their own feelings. It's OK for other people to have feelings, and it's OK for you to have them, as well.

Empathy Creates Long-Lasting Friendships

Sympathy means that you feel sorry for someone else because of something that happened to them. However, sympathy comes from a distance. You feel sorry for children in the world who are hungry. You might also feel sorry for someone in the grade above you in school who is sick. However, when it comes to those close to you, you want to express more than just sympathy. If you really, really care about them and love them, you want to understand how they feel from their point of view. What would it be like to be them in a bad situation? This is an old Native American saying: "Never criticize a man unless you've walked a mile in their moccasins."

When people say they're having a problem or in a bad situation, most people say something like this: "Oh, you **shouldn't** feel that way." As said in Chapter 3, *"shouldn't"* is one of those words that are associated with anxiety. It's a negative word. Perhaps your friend shouldn't feel bad, *but the fact remains that she does.* Telling her she shouldn't feel bad rejects her right to have her own feeling. Your friend most likely already knows that, but you reminding her doesn't make the feeling go away. Everyone's feelings matter.

What you can do is to say you understand that they're feeling bad, and you're sorry that they feel that way. "I wish I could make that bad feeling go away." You might suggest going to the store for some ice cream and talking about it. Encourage your friend to dump more feelings on you. They need to get it out of their system, and you might be the only person who permits them to do that. Just that alone will help, because you're "walking in their moccasins" with them. They are no longer alone with their bad feeling.

This takes time, patience, and sacrifice. It isn't pleasant to do this; you'd prefer to go home. You have other things to do. But look at the beauty of what you have done for the other person. It speaks well for you.

"Hurt People Hurt People"

This is an old saying. What it means is that, if a person is really upset, they might try to blame you or anybody else for their upset. They're not really angry with you (unless you give them reason). They're frustrated because things aren't going well with them. They're also feeling very insecure. Hurting back doesn't work. If you try to get an idea of how the other feels, then you're practicing empathy. If you can bring yourself to feel some compassion for the other, you'll be loved and admired for your maturity.

Remember that most of your friends and schoolmates have good intentions. That will do a lot toward helping you resolve issues and be of help to others. There are people with whom you can't get along. That doesn't mean that they don't deserve the same courtesy your friends do. We're all in this world together, and we strive to make it a warm and comfortable place. Treat others like you want to be treated.

Criticism

"Criticism" is almost a bad word, isn't it? That's the tough part of being a teen. You're not quite an adult, so your parents, your teachers, and other adults in your life correct you. They're still trying to guide you like they did when you were a little kid...or at least it feels like that. It's a difficult time when you're in-between being a kid and being an adult. Besides, you make mistakes, even when you don't intend to.

You know, a lot of adults look at what's wrong instead

of what's right. They often forget to tell you when you're doing well. That's because the whole world has a negative bias. Besides, adults feel like they're still responsible for you. It makes you feel like you want to be an adult in a couple of seconds, and be able to live in your own place and earn your own money. What should you do when you feel offended that these adults don't trust you?

1. Try telling yourself that they are sharing their opinion with you. In reality, they don't know how mature you are, but want to be sure you do OK.
2. Consider the fact that the other person might be right. They might be giving you the correct advice. It's hard to admit it, but you really could be wrong.
3. You—and only you—can choose to be hurt by criticism. After all, you can just simply shrug your shoulders and take it as a well-intentioned remark.

You are a good and valuable person. What criticism others have for you will never, ever subtract from your goodness as a human being. If your little brother is putting on his shirt wrong, you might suggest to him as to how to do it correctly. That's constructive criticism. It doesn't mean he's not a valuable person or undeserving of love. The same thing goes for you. When someone offers you constructive criticism, it doesn't mean you're stupid.

Life on the Phone

The 21st century is most challenging. There are pressures upon you from all over the place. Your cell phone is convenient. It's nice, too, because you can get information and you can text or talk to your friends without having to visit them.

Did you know that teens touch their cell phones 150 times a day? You also get tons and tons of notifications and ads. The average teen spends about seven hours a day on their cell phones. Isn't that astonishing?

Adults have the same problem, too. There was once a woman who was walking along the sidewalk tapping furiously on her cell phone. She didn't see a water fountain in front of her, then tripped over the edge, and fell in! *Splash!* They showed a video of this on the Internet and then on TV. Can you imagine how embarrassed she was?!

This chapter is about active listening. Cell phones have a sneaky way of hiding the reactions of others. Suppose a guy you know texts you. Let's say that he likes you and is trying to get a date. Guys and girls are shy when it comes to starting up new relationships. You have to tread carefully. Now, if your new admirer is texting you, it's hard to tell what they're feeling. If you see their face, they might be smiling coyly. Then you would know. Text is just that—text. Just words on a screen. Black against white or blue.

Why not try a little courage and ask if you two could meet somewhere to talk? If they agree, you'll get a clue as to how they feel. Emojis are helpful, but they don't tell you the whole story.

The "Likes"

In the "old days," it wasn't important to have "likes" on your phone, or "friend requests" from other sites. Today, with peer pressure as it is, people expect that you have a lot of "likes" and a lot of "friends." They're like badges of honor. Many of those friend requests, by the way, are from people you don't even know! You're also pressured into looking your absolute best when you send someone a photo of yourself. All of this digital activity expected of you gives you a pressure you don't need. The "online world" is much different than the real world.

The cell phone is a device—a tool. It's not how you'll be remembered by your friends and relatives. Besides, when someone asks how many "likes" you have, you can say you have a lot, but you don't know how many. Do they have the time to check up on you? No. They're too busy taking care of their own digital world.

If you don't have many "likes," it does *NOT* mean no one likes you. "Like" is an emotion. You do have people who like you. Whether they plug it into their cell phones or not won't ever change that.

Chapter 9 – Trouble

Trouble: Easy to Get Into; Tough to Get Out Of

Mick's Gang

Mick used to hang around with the guys in the town. He thought they were cool, and they treated him well. They played games at the video arcade and they invited him when they went for hamburgers. He was the youngest in the group, and this made him feel important.

One day Alex, one of the guys, asked Mick to give a guy at #36 Vreeland Avenue a bag. "I have to leave, so I'd appreciate it if you could give this to him."

"OK," Mick replied.

Mick delivered the bag to the guy at the door.

Later on, Alex asked Mick to help with delivering more of those bags. No problem.

On one Wednesday, Mick and the guys were walking down the street. Mick was talking to Alex while they went down the street. Then he asked Alex a question. No answer.

Mick looked over toward Alex, but Alex had disappeared. Mick looked around some more and saw all the guys hiding down some stairs that led to a basement apartment. As Mick turned toward the street, he saw a police car go by. 'Why was everybody hiding?' he wondered.

After the cop car passed, the guys joined him. This was very strange behavior.

Later on, Mick discovered why the guys were acting strangely. Mick was carrying drugs to people in the area. When he got worried about it, they reassured him, and even gave him some money. Wow! All he had to do was that?

After a few months of doing that, the guys started asking him to do other things. Like stealing a jacket from the store. "I'm not going to able to do that!" he complained.

"Sure, you can," said Alex. "It's easy. Just get the jacket and hang out by the 'In' door. As soon as someone comes in, the door will swing open. Then you run out of the 'In' door. Nobody will notice."

Mick was nervous about that, but he did it and no one caught him. The guys praised him and told him he was now a junior "gang" member.

When Mick realized what happened, and discovered that he was also carrying drugs to people in those little bags, he got scared and wanted out.

Mick had been so thrilled he had a group of guys to hang out with, but now he was afraid he'd go to jail. He wanted out of the gang. What was he going to do?

There are solutions, but they have to be handled correctly:

Some suggestions:

- Don't make any statements about leaving the gang.
- Spend less and less time hanging out with the gang. Make excuses, like you have to go someplace with your father.
- Try joining local sports teams or art groups and the

like.

- Change your appearance. Wear very different clothes so you won't be recognized.
- Try to hang out with other kids, even the girls.
- Change you email address and your cell phone number.
- If you talk to your guidance counselor, he or she might have some people you can talk to that can help you get out of the gang. There may be gang and crime prevention units in your town. There are also hotlines listed on the Internet which can offer some assistance.

The Makeup Jamboree

The girls from the school always collected in cliques. Girls that were not in the cliques weren't accepted, so they went elsewhere on the weekends. Meghan, though, got lucky one day:

True Story: Meghan's Makeup

Peg, from one of the girls' cliques, invited Meghan to her house with the other girls after school one day. They were going to have a "makeover." Everybody was going to play

---

with new makeup that Peg had bought from the store. Meghan normally wasn't part of this "in" group, so she was excited. Then Peg drove Meghan and the other girls over to her house. It was exciting. They had all kinds of makeup, perfumes, and even wigs. Meghan, though, knew that her mother expected her home. Meghan decided right then and there that she wasn't going to call her mother. Her mother wouldn't let her stay, she figured. So she just stayed. The day was really fun. Meghan looked terrific in her new makeup. Her skin color looked great, and her eye makeup made her look like those actresses on TV. Meghan learned how to properly use eyeliner.

Suddenly, it started to get dark. Meghan asked Peg to drive her home, but Peg couldn't do it. She had to go to her aunt's. The other girls had rides, too...all except Meghan. Uh oh! So, Meghan called home. There was no answer...only the answering machine. Her mom's cell phone was all full, so Meghan couldn't leave a message. Then Meghan started walking home. It was a little over a mile.

Meghan realized what she did wrong, but it was too late. She started walking. As night was coming close, Meghan spotted her mother's car. Her mother pulled up. Boy! Meghan thought her Mom would be furious, but she wasn't. There were tears in her eyes, and she was frantic.

Meghan climbed in the car, and her mother hugged her and hugged her. "I almost called the police!" she cried.

Regardless of how rocky your relationships are with your parents, they will stand behind you and help you get out of jams. Trust in the old saying, "Blood is thicker than water." Your connection with your parents is a bond. Meghan did have to sit though some long lectures by her mother, but she didn't mind them as much this time. She knew that she was loved.

Chapter 10 – Happiness On and Off

The Love "Potions"

What triggers your automatic attraction to another? In your brain, there are bio-chemicals that are set off when you're drawn to another. They're called "dopamine," and "oxytocin." They're also called the "pleasure hormones." When those hormones are circulated throughout your body, they make you feel attracted to someone. Beyond the biological process involved, your cognition is involved, of course. That's the spark that lights the flame, and the rest follows as it has from the beginning of time.

After that, the mere presence of the other who'll light up your life will thrill you. The most difficult part of this process is the physical meeting. First of all, you scout around, asking his or her friends about him/her. Then you'll ask if they've ever said anything about you. It can be a disappointment if they never mentioned you. That can be fixed. Do your "geography." What's that mean? It consists of maneuvering yourself in such a way that the other sees you— by standing near their locker, standing near his or her friends while they're talking, and making yourself noticeable. The bravest among you will ask a question or two…probably about some movie or rock group. If they don't strike up a conversation, you're not stuck. You can ask questions about what teachers he/she likes or doesn't like. Small talk. Yet, the best introduction of all is simple: " Hi." Say it with a smile, and look at them straight in the eyes. Then start with questions about him/her. Avoid talking about yourself if you can. This is about him or her- not you. You have now peaked their curiosity.

How Can You Tell This Might Be a Good Relationship?

<u>Respect</u>

Is he or she respectful? Sometimes the other starts out with a joke. Don't get turned off. Humor can be a nervous response.

<u>Listening</u>

Does the other listen to you…really listen? Are they entertaining? Do you like his or her looks? Don't refrain from making a nice comment about some physical feature.

<u>Similar Interests</u>

Here's a chance for your first date. Ask them about their interests. What do they do for fun? Are they involved in sports? What rock groups or movie stars do they like? You can suggest that the two of you go to a movie you both like.

<u>The Tricky First Date</u>

Someone has to break the tension of wondering if there's any chance of love. Usually, it's the one who gets to the point where he/she is ready to explode and has to reach out. Safe places are usually best in the beginning. The ice cream shop. The mall. A movie.

Some people make mistakes in the beginning. You almost can't help it, because you're very taken with the other person. You're insatiably curious; you want to know what they're doing all the time. Keep the mystery of you alive. By all means, cast a glance their way and smile. It shows you're still interested. One of the biggest mistakes a person can make is to text them too frequently. "Uh oh," they'll think. Is she/he a pest? Another mistake is following them around a lot. You don't want to be thought of as a puppy dog, after all, but you secretly wish you could.

"I Love You"

Love isn't just that warm and fuzzy feeling they write songs about. Do you like other things about that person? Do you have similar likes and dislikes? Can you carry on a private conversation without making out? Yes! You should be able to. Love should include all the elements friendship does. It evokes conversations about just about anything. Be sure to talk about the interests of the other, and get involved in those things if possible. In the beginning, it's best to pick public places. You'll want to touch and make out, so privacy will be sought. Feel the intensity of your touching so you can guide the relationship with regard as to whether or not you want to pursue sex. Most teens don't leap into bed early on. Others do, of course, but this level of intimacy is best to discuss in advance. If a friend tells you they're already having sex, you need not believe them. Some do it to brag, and not one iota of it is true. This is a decision only the two of you can make.

Sex

Having sex will change your relationship. Think long and hard about it before crossing that line. There are also choices you need to make—adult choices—and many of you might be confused about it. Be careful...very careful. If someone just cares about your looks and not your personality or your interests, nor your dreams for the future, he or she is just interested in your body.

The Hard Facts:

1. Biologically, boys can get aroused easily when they feel drawn to you. It's not a moral failing; they have little control over it, as it is perfectly natural. You should never be forced to have sex if you don't feel ready for it. When the issue comes up, let him know your feelings. Avoid situations which may put you into a compromising position, like going into a deserted area to make out.

2. Refrain from believing all the advice from your peers. Ask a trusted adult instead.

3. If you do feel ready, realize this—you may get pregnant. There are precautions you can take to prevent that like birth control pills, diaphragms, or condoms. Pregnancy, of course, may lead to birth. Giving up your child for adoption is another choice, but a painful one.

Keeping the child is a tremendous responsibility. It can mean that you may not be able to establish a career, as babies take a lot of time and money. Holding a regular job will be difficult at best in the future. Realize that your mother will have to do a lot of babysitting to help out. She may or may not be ready or able to do that.

You will automatically love your baby, but don't look to the baby to fill all your needs for affection. He or she can't do that. In addition, it isn't wise to have a child in order to get your boyfriend to marry you. He may not do that, or may make a lousy husband if neither of you are really, really ready.

Some teens date just to "show off" their partner. That's no foundation for a meaningful relationship. The other isn't a showpiece, they're a person. Watch how they treat other people. Are they polite? If you two have a disagreement, how is it resolved? That's very important. Do you have some misgivings about them? That is, there is an intuition that there are "snakes in their head." That means, is there a part of the other that always seems mysterious, or do they change the topic of conversation when you bring something up?

You may want to change something about the other. That is a mistake. Most people—teens and adults—don't change drastically. It's taken each person years to develop and grow their personality, and it's not easy to change. Everyone has limitations. If they have a bad habit, the wisest thing to do is to learn to put up with it. Just remind yourself that you, too, are imperfect. If your partner has an intolerable habit like becoming drunk, your inner warning light will go off. You may have to end the relationship.

Once you love someone, you are vulnerable, but through vulnerability comes strength. You want things to always be as they are now. In this changing world, that doesn't always happen. The truth of the matter is the fact that you will grow together or grow apart. Love is a risk, but you will become a far better person for taking that risk.

"'Tis better to have loved and lost, than never to have loved at all."

The above quote is from Alfred Lord Tennyson, and speaks to the beauty of love. Love is magnificent, and there is nothing in the world that can compare to that.

Your partner will always like other people. That's normal. It's how they deal with it that may or may not present a challenge in your relationship. If you were to overreact, you might start smothering the other. That, of course, is a real "turn-off." If your partner starts straying, what's your choice? You have none! That's a sobering statement to make, but a relationship is built on trust. Your partner may fall in love with someone other than you and end the relationship. It's painful, but that's life. That sounds very sobering, doesn't it? Besides that, two people who are close will most likely know it before it happens, simply through sheer intuition. There will be dark clouds in your sky, and you will do anything and everything to escape their shadows.

This isn't a one-sided matter, though. You may also be wildly attracted to someone else. The most mature way to deal with that is to talk about it before the other is deeply hurt by discovering it through happenstance or from a classmate.

The importance of discussing a pending break-up is easy to say and easy to write. In reality though, there's nothing easy about it.

Break-Ups

If the two of you break up, there's always a "loser" whose heart will be broken. You will cry and scream. You will call, you will text, and silence will be the response. You'll write letters, more letters, and poems as an emotional outlet. There's an old adage, "Time heals all wounds." You've probably heard it, but thinking of that doesn't matter, does it? Although it sounds silly, find distractions. That won't heal your hurt, so it's a waiting game. Such is the way of pain.

The Perennial See-Saw of Happy and Sad

There are times of sadness, when your mind's voice will call out and the only voice that answers will be your own. Throughout this book, there are tips and tricks for making yourself happy. But, let's face it, who's ever gotten happy because someone told them to? There will be times when you're confronted with a problem, when you're absorbed with a negative thought you can't shake, and when somebody says something mean to you. It seems that everywhere you look you see those smiley stickers, as if they're magic charms. You can't buy into all of this, because it's not true all the time. There are unhappy times; there are times when you'll feel frustration and anger; there are times when you'll feel sadness and fear; and there will be times of disappointment and guilt.

As human beings, we all need to learn that unhappy thoughts will come our way, no matter how hard we try to shove them aside. Sometimes, when you obsess on getting rid of a negative thought, it sticks in your head like glue. If you start thinking that your thoughts define you, that isn't true.

Everyone, especially you teens, wants to learn how to deal with those negative thoughts. Well, for one thing, it's helpful if you accept the fact that you're feeling negative. It could be a bad hair day; it could be a day that your friends are in bad moods; it could be a day that you're grounded. Stuff happens. You'll get over them and other people will, too. How many times, after you've finished with your period of being grounded, it's like nothing happened? That takes the sting out of it instantly.

You're Supposed to Have Bad Feelings Sometimes

They say you're supposed to overcome bad thoughts and negative times. Otherwise, *they* say those bad thoughts will control you. Really? Just who said that, anyway? The great "They's" of the world? Those are those people discussed in Chapter 1. They are the nameless and faceless, who supposedly feel they have a calling to run your life. Well, the great "They" doesn't seem to understand that *you're* the boss of *you* and "They" aren't! You can let those negative thoughts get you down. However, that doesn't mean that you're always going to have those thoughts and always going to feel down. Those thoughts don't control you. **You control *you*.** Just because you're having a bad day, doesn't mean all your days will be bad.

Remember in Chapter 5, you tried out some of those Mindfulness Mediations. You let thoughts come into your mind, but then let them drift away. The same is true of your negative thoughts and feelings. You can let them come and go.

Notice the adults around you. Also take note of people you admire. They all have difficult times, but it doesn't kill them. They get through it. Unhappiness is part of life. Feelings aren't "right" or "wrong." Repeat: *Feelings aren't "right" or "wrong."* They're feelings—that's all. They're inside your brain. What counts is what you do with them. You can punch somebody in the face, but you don't have to.

There is a skill to expressing your feelings in such a way that they're not painful for someone else. When you object to something someone said, practice talking about *your own* feelings first. For example, "*I felt bad* when you said _____." You can also say: "I was confused when you said _____." You can also put on a face of shock and lapse into silence. The other will get the idea. In the case of bullies (or narcissists) sometimes just holding a straight face works, and it's a challenge to keep that up (but it can be done).

When you feel bad, yes, you can share that feeling with a friend. However, there's no need to apologize for having that feeling. What if you went around spending a lot of your time apologizing? You'd then be telling yourself and telling other people that you don't measure up. Of course, if you've really hurt someone's feelings, apologize, but leave your apologizing to that. You certainly don't need to apologize for having needs, nor for asking for things. You don't need to apologize for who you are. You're a good and amazing person and deserve respect and love.

Your Undiscovered Skill

As you move through your teenage years, pay close attention. Did you know you have a special skill NO ONE else has?! The comedian, Jim Carrey, for example, has a "rubber face," and made a lot of money on it. Take a look at Skip and Treena's Experiences:

True Story: Talents

Skip spent a lot of time in his backyard. It was in a suburban area. Whenever he saw a groundhog or a chipmunk, he investigated. He put his nose a few inches above the ground, and suddenly discovered he could smell them! Yes, it's true. When he went downstairs to his basement, he smelled

---

something weird. Upon investigation, he found out that what he smelled were crickets! In his yard, Skip found new smells. When he just leaned down a bit he could smell an area where deer had recently passed through. He could smell pond water. He could even smell bears (Yikes!).

When he went to a local nature preserve, the same thing happened. Skip started thinking that he had picked up on a talent that the Native Americans had. The olfactory sense has long been neglected in today's world, but not overlooked by Skip. In the years that followed, Skip became a guide for one of the National Parks in America.

Treena has a different special skill. When she worked for a bakery, she was able to decorate cakes with complex and beautiful designs—so beautiful that you almost didn't want to eat the cake! People lined up all the way down the block and around the corner. She could "draw people's faces" on cakes; she would design forests and flowers, dresses with lace and crowns, and even wild tornadoes! Because of her skill, the bakery expanded and she had her own wing. It was a very lucrative position.

Surely, you've heard of guys who can fix your car, even though they had no training in it. You've seen robot cars that are really wild and partake in competitions. You may have even heard of musicians that can play like maestros, but they can't read music!

Why don't you look into yourself for a hidden talent? It could be fun; it could be weird; it could be hideous; it could be a special gift no one else you know has.

Spend your time searching for your own special skill.

Colleges and Your Rediscovered Parents

When you're an older teen—around 17—your room is piled up with college applications. This may come as a shock, but it isn't absolutely necessary that you go to college the following year. Vocational schools are available, and should likewise be researched. You might have been a whiz in your auto mechanics' class. You may have had a job working with an electrician, a builder, or a plumber and would like to study that. Emotionally, you may not feel ready for college. There's no reason why you can't put it off for a year or two. Talk about that with your parents, as difficult as it may be. Some young people enter college, have a traumatic period of adjustment, and drop out. It's best to avoid that.

In other cases, your parents may own a business they want to train you in. Of course, it's crucial that you, too, like the work, but this opportunity is a great one.

For those of you who are considering college, there will be tests you have to take. Tutors are available to help prepare you. Take advantage of them. According to the 19th century psychologist, Hermann Ebbinghaus, a huge amount of the factual information you learned will be forgotten within seven days. So, if you're smart, don't fall back on your IQ to save the day. It's your memory, not your IQ, that counts on achievement tests. Other tests may be given to test your IQ, depending upon the college.

Some general advice to think about and discuss with your parents:

- Costs of tuition (financial aid is available)
- Size of the college – Some teens aren't comfortable with a huge campus and a large student body. Others flourish in that atmosphere.
- Don't go to a "party school" – You won't have enough time to study, the dorms will be noisy, and you may be sucked into an under-culture of drinking and drugs. Keep in mind that older students can be very

persuasive. And, guys, they will be larger than you.

- Sports is a consideration if you have a favorite one and/or one in which you're talented.

- If you have an interest in art, music, TV production, hotel management, business or theater, look for a college that features that as one of its majors. They will have a lot of equipment and technology which can prepare you to enter those fields professionally.

College: The Nature of Your Relationship With Your Parents Changes

Once you and your parents start discussing your future schooling, whether college or vocational school, they will change. This event is just as traumatic for them as it is for you. Feelings will be high on the part of both your parents. Your parents will give you advice…perhaps until you're weary of it. They will feel compelled to stuff everything you will need to know about life into a few hours. Be patient with them. That'll be difficult for you. However, realize that your parents are nervous and afraid. They visualize you leaving them. They visualize your empty room. They picture you with a lot of new friends who will shut them out.

Return to Chapter 8 and reread the section on

empathy. Now it's time to practice it on your parents, which is a jolting experience. As for you, you feel exhilarated, so you'll have to pretend a lot. You can't wait to be free! You can't wait to make all your own decisions, while your parents are in fear and trepidation that you'll make the wrong ones.

At age 18, you're no longer a child. However, a parent is always a parent.

To assert yourself, be sure to act like an adult with them. Find humor wherever you can. There are interests that you shared with your mother and father. Try to keep those alive. Yes, you may have to "pay your dues" and visit them. They'll help you out when you need them. Your mom is going to give you cookies and sweets—a lot more than she used to. Do a few nice things for them when you can. Do tell them about your experiences at college or vocational school.

If you have problems, try to share them. After all, as an adult, you share those with friends, and parents, too, want to be your friends. Of course, you can reject their advice, but try not to let on. They may also have sound advice, so give them the courtesy of active listening. They, too, left their parents once upon a time and know what it feels like. No, it may not have happened in the digital world you live in, but humans are humans throughout the centuries. Human behavior hasn't changed much over the years.

Retrograde Motion

Remember all those arguments you were involved in when you were younger? Be prepared. They will crop up again, and you'll be very tempted to respond to them the way you used to. Now that you're 17 or 18, surely you've developed more mature ways of responding. Sometimes it may call for just shutting your mouth. Don't get sucked into the old times. Besides, your younger sisters and brothers will want to look up to you, so you need to act differently. This is hard to do.

Your parents may not respect all of your decisions, and will tell you so. There may even be topics that you don't want to express to them. It's now time to set boundaries, but in a calm way. Just tell them that those topics may cause hard feelings and lead to conflicts, so you'd rather not talk about them. This isn't disobedience; it's the mature way to handle issues that can set either of you off.

The "Inspection Team"

When you're in college, be ready for the "Royal Visit!"

(Your parents' visit, that is.) Be sure to warn them ahead of time that they cannot simply "drop in" whenever they feel like it. Schedule a day and time (with an ending time). You know what they want to do, especially your mother—the usual things like making sure your room is tidy, dirty dishes aren't piled up in the sink, the microwave is clean, and you have an area designated to study. If you have a roommate, warn him or her well in advance. Be sure your place is neat...even neater than it ever was at home. Stuff the dirty clothes under the bed, if you need to!

Tour the campus with them. Introduce them to any professors you may meet. Parents are very impressed by that. Say hello to the new friends you've made, and introduce your parents. Your friends know what you know—that you're trying to make a good impression, so they'll behave well. When your parents meet your friends, they will be pleased that you have them.

Limits

In some families where there was a great deal of conflict, you may feel the need to limit your visits home. Such was the case with Brianna:

153

Brianna's Fiery Relationship With Her Mom

Brianna loved her mom, but the two of them argued vociferously for years. Her dad was the reserved type and never partook in those arguments. When Brianna visited home from college, everything went smoothly for the first few hours. Then Mom started making critical comments. For a year prior to her departure for college, Brianna had practiced trying to control her own reactions, but only with limited success. Now that she was in college, she realized that conflicts might arise when she visited home. Brianna knew she could hold her temper in check, but not for long. When she visited, she decided to stay just for a day and a half on the weekend.

Her father was genuinely sad and upset that she wasn't going to stay longer. Brianna felt terrible about that. In private, she discussed the issue with him:

"Dad, you know how Mom and I always used to fight. I don't want that to keep happening. Mom says things that she knows upsets me. She 'pushes all my buttons.' I can take that without complaint until around Sunday morning. I love you and would like to stay longer, but things will only get uncomfortable for all of us if I go beyond my limit." Her father lapsed into silence, but he understood.

If You Live at Home

If you stay at home, your mother and father will try to continue servicing you as they did before. However, if you're working, it is better that you contribute. Some parents and their teen children have a "rental situation," whereby the teen pays the parents for their share of food, laundry, etc. This shows that you are becoming a responsible adult. There needs to be a discussion about the hours you keep, and what works out for everyone. Most parents object if you have your boyfriend/girlfriend overnight in your bedroom. That issue must be addressed.

You have a right to privacy in your room. This is a tricky issue, as your parents may want to "snoop" when you're out. Decide how you're going to handle that issue. "Helicopter parents" are parents who will want to know what you're up to much of the time. It comes from their well-intentioned concerns, but is inappropriate. Again, such issues need to be resolved in a calm and caring fashion. As for your social media involvements, don't permit them entry. Don't befriend them on Facebook or other sites.

155

Your parents have a strong need now to develop new interests. It would be better for them to develop their own interests outside of the home. They now need your help and guidance.

Have your own routines and schedules. Limit your availability. Act as if you're a renter in their home. Try not to prance around the house half-dressed, and keep your things out of their space.

Do spend time with them, though. Like the parents whose teens are at college, they want time to "visit" with you.

You love them and you are loved by them. Maintain that always.

Conclusion

This little book has touched on most of the issues that surface when you're nearing that horizon of adulthood. Adulthood is just over the ridge, but you can't see what lies beyond. Your future is awash in red and purple hues that hover above the beautiful horizon. Your life is beautiful and it's exciting. Your greatest challenge is trying to get yourself there unscathed.

It's your life and you are in control of you. You have free will to make the choices you feel are important. There will be exciting times during your teens, but there will be those nasty down times as well. We, human beings, are all flawed. To expect more than that is foolish. The singer, Taylor Swift, once sang about wishing "you could go back and tell yourself what you know now."

In this book, exercises are delineated to help you get through this tender time of your life. Reasons for the disruptions in your life during this crucial time were explained, along with these words of encouragement you should remember always—you are truly a unique and amazing person.

In all the world, there is none like you, and that's something you can be proud of.

Bibliography

"12 Science-Based Benefits of Meditation" Retrieved from https://www.healthline.com/nutrition/12-benefits-of-meditation

"What is Mindfulness?" Retrieved from https://www.mindful.org/what-is-mindfulness/

Kabat-Zinn, J. "Mindfulness Meditation" Retrieved from https://www.mindfulnesscds.com/pages/about-the-author

"Physiology, Cortisol" Retrieved from https://www.ncbi.nlm.nih.gov/books/NBK538239/

"How to Balance your Stress Hormones with Carbs" Retrieved from http://www.allgreatnutrition.com/blog/nutrition-tips-for-anxiety-carbohydrates#:~:text=Whole%2C%20minimally%20processed%2C%20complex%20carbohydrates,it%20calms%20the%20stress%20response.

"Foods That Help Tame Stress" Retrieved from https://www.webmd.com/diet/ss/slideshow-diet-for-stress-management

"Science Says Stress is Contagious—Here's How to Avoid Catching It" Retrieved from https://www.healthline.com/health-news/stress-cues-from-others

"Symptoms of Stress" Retrieved from https://saylordotorg.github.io/text_human-relations/s07-02-symptoms-of-stress.html

"5 Ways Social Media Affects Teen Mental Health" Retrieved from https://www.verywellfamily.com/ways-social-media-affects-teen-mental-health-4144769

Fitzsimmons, K. (2021) *Teen's Guide: Social Skills for Teens.* Rockridge Press

Meurisse, T. (2018) Master Your Emotions. Kindle.

Carnegie, D. (2010) How to Win Friends and Influence People. Simon & Shuster

Birch, K. "How Social Media Affects the Mental Health of Teenagers"

Meyers, K & Briggs, I. "Free Personality Test" Retrieved from https://www.16personalities.com/free-personality-test

"Personality Test" Retrieved from http://www.humanmetrics.com/cgi-win/jtypes2.asp

Cherry, K. "The 5 Levels of Maslow's Hierarchy of Needs" Retrieved from https://www.verywellmind.com/what-is-maslows-hierarchy-of-needs-4136760

"How to Leave a Gang." Retrieved from https://www.ydinm.org/2020/05/20/how-to-leave-a-gang/

Made in the USA
Las Vegas, NV
15 July 2021

26460267R00089